National transposition measures
Situation at 1st January 1998

98

Employment & social affairs

European Commission

Secretariat-General / Directorate-General for Employment,
Industrial Relations and Social Affairs - Unit V/1

Manuscript completed in December 1997.

The contents of this publication do not necessarily reflect the opinion or position of the European Commission.

The information in this publication is also available in the SCADPLUS database on the EUROPA server at the following address:
http://europa.eu.int/comm/sg/scadplus/

A great deal of additional information on the European Union is available on the Internet. It can be accessed through the Europa server (http://europa.eu.int).

Cataloguing data can be found at the end of this publication.

Luxembourg: Office for Official Publications of the European Communities, 1998

ISBN 92-828-2747-X

Printed in Belgium

TABLE OF CONTENTS

Foreword - Pàdraig Flynn

1. Labour law and working conditions

2. Equality of opportunity for women and men

3. Free movement for workers

4. Health and safety at work

5. Public health

NATIONAL MEASURES TRANSPOSING SOCIAL DIRECTIVES

Most laws in the field of social affairs and the labour market are of national origin. Nevertheless, in an increasingly integrated Union, there is an important body of legislation at Community level. Social provision at European level has, as one of its primary concerns, the building of a truly European labour market which respects the social aspirations articulated in Article 2 of the EC Treaty. It has, therefore, four logical manifestations: equal opportunities; free movement of workers; health and safety and public health; and classic labour law.

To date, 64 Directives have been adopted covering these aspects, of which 52 have come into force. Their transposition into national law is fundamental to the reality of making Community rights accessible to individuals and creating a level playing field for competition in the increasingly integrated Single Market. The measures aim to minimise the potential for conflict of interest and distortion of competition and to enable the full potential of the developing market in goods, services and labour to be secured.

As this second edition of our situation report on *"National measures transposing social Directives"* shows, the process of translating these Directives into national regulatory frameworks is being achieved. The purpose of this publication is to ensure transparency in the process of transposition. Nevertheless, the tables refer only to national measures adopted to transpose Community Law and give no indication as to whether Laws have been fully complied with. The latter is now our main priority and we are currently checking whether each Member State has correctly transposed each Directive.

This second edition is appearing in nine languages and uses a sharper format to improve clarity and accessibility of the information.

I recommend it to you, as a tool for understanding and monitoring the progress of putting in place the crucial aspects of creating a well functioning European Union market for workers, as well as for the goods and services sectors. The European Commission, and particularly DG V, the Directorate-General for *"Employment, Industrial Relations and Social Affairs"*, remain at your service for any questions or comments you have on the content of this publication.

Pàdraig FLYNN

IMPROVED LIVING AND WORKING CONDITIONS

Collective redundancies

Council Directive 75/129/EEC of 17 February 1975 on the approximation of the laws of the Member States relating to collective redundancies.

Council Directive 92/56/EEC of 24 June 1992 amending Directive 75/129/EEC on the approximation of the laws of the Member States relating to collective redundancies.

1) Deadline for implementation of the legislation in the Member States

Directive 75/129/EEC: 19.02.1977

Directive 92/56/EEC: 24.06.1994

2) References

Official Journal L 48, 22.02.1975

Official Journal L 245, 26.08.1992

A	Arbeitsmarktförderungsgesetz (AMFG)§45a Arbeitsvertragsrechtsanpassung Änderung Arbeitsverfassung Gesetz vom 01/06/95 zur Änderung der Landarbeitsordnung 1985	Bundesgesetzblatt N.18/1993 Bundesgesetzblatt N.459/1993 Bundesgesetzblatt N.460/1993 Landesgesetzblatt für Kärnten N.69/85, 25/08/95

B	Convention Collective de Travail N.10 du 08/05/73, modifié par A.R.du 06/08/73 Convention Collective de Travail - CCT N.24 du 02/10/75 modifié le 06/12/83 et par A.R. du 07/02/84 Arrêté Royal du/Koninklijk Besluit van 21/01/76 Arrêté Royal du 24/05/76 modifié par A.R. du 26/03/84 et 11/06/86 Koninklijk Besluit van 24/05/76, tot wijziging van het K.B. van 26/03/84 en 11/06/86 Convention Collective de Travail N.24 du	Moniteur Belge du/Belgisch Staatsblad van 17/2/76 Moniteur Belge du/Belgisch Staatsblad van 17/9/76

	08/10/85, modifié par A.R. du 20/12/85 Arrêté Royal du/Koninklijk Besluit van 11/06/86 Arrêté Royal du/Koninklijk Besluit van 28/2/94 Convention collective CNT N.24, 21.12.93 Arrêté Royal du/Koninklijk Besluit van 9/3/93	Moniteur Belge du/Belgisch Staatsblad van 15/01/86 Moniteur belge Moniteur belge du/Belgisch Staatsblad van 28/3/93, reg 7739

D	Kündigungsschutzgesetz, 25/08/69 Gesetz vom 27/04/78 zur Änderung der KündigungsG, 13/07/88 Gesetz zur anpassung arbeitsrechtlicher Bestimmungen andas EG-recht vom 20/7/95	Bundesgesetzblatt Teil I, p.1317, 1969 Bundesgesetzblatt Teil I, p.1037, 29/04/78 Bundesgesetzblatt (Teile I, II, III) NR.38 vom 27/7/95 s.947

DK	Lov N.38, 26/01/77 Cirkulære fra Arbejdsministeriet, 04/03/77 Dekret fra Arbejdsministeriet, N.73, 04/03/77 Dekret fra Arbejdsministeriet, N.755, 12/11/90 Lov N.414 af 24/6/94	Ministerialtidende 4.KT. j.nr. 11300-8, 01/04/77 Ministerialtidende 4 KT. j.nr. 11300-8, 04/03/77 Ministerialtidende 4 KT.N.11.300 8 1

E	Ley 8/1980, 10/03/80 (Estatuto de los Trabajadores-ET) (Article 51) Real Decreto N.696/80, 14/04/80 Ley N.11/94, 19/05/94	Boletín Oficial del Estado 14/03/80 Boletín Oficial del Estado 14/04/80 Boletín Oficial del Estado N.122, p.15805, 23/05/94

EL	Loi N.1387 du 19/07/83	

F	Code du Travail Art.L.321-3 avis 321-12 Loi N.75-5, 03/01/75 Décret N.75-326, 05/05/75 Arrêté ministériel, 25/06/75 Circulaire N.27/75 Décret N.76-295 Loi du 02/08/89 (n.89-549) (Articles L. 122-14, L. 123-3-1,L.132-12, L. 132-27, L. 143-11, L.321- 1 à L. 321-15, L.322-1, L.322-3, L. 322-7 et autres du Code du Travail Loi n°92/722 du 29/7/92	Journal Officiel, 04/01/75 Journal Officiel, 04/04/75 Journal Officiel, 07/05/75 Journal Officiel, 01/07/75 Journal Officiel, 02/07/75 Journal Officiel, 06/04/76
FIN	Laki yhteistoiminnasta yrityksissä (725/78,22/08/78, muutos(236/93), 26/02/93 Työsopimuslaki (320/70), 30/04/70, muutos (1354/93), 22/12/93	
I	Legge N.223 (Art.24), 23 luglio 1991	Gazzetta Ufficiale N.175, p.3, 27 luglio 1991
IRL	Protection of Employment Act 1977 Protection of Employment Act 1977 (Notification of Proposed Collective Redundancies) Reg. 1977 Protection of Employment Order of 1996	Irof, 30/03/77, Statutory Instrument, 10/05/77 Statutory Instrument N.140, 1977 Statutory Instruments n.370 of 1996
L	Arrêté Grand Ducal, 30/06/45 Arrêté Grand Ducal, 30/10/58 Loi, 24/06/70 Loi, 28/07/73 Loi, 26/07/75 Loi, 02/03/82 Loi, 14/05/86 Loi du 23/07/93	Mémorial, 12/07/45 Mémorial, 17/11/58 Mémorial A N.35, 30/06/70 Mémorial A N.46, 14/08/73 Mémorial A N.46, 31/07/75 Memorial A N.54, p.1073, 28/07/93

NL	Wet, 24/03/76 Wet tot wijziging 1971 Minesteriele Verordening, 17/11/76 Wet van 07/07/93 Besluit van 13/09/93	Staatsblad N.223, 24/03/76 Staatsblad N.625, 30/11/76 Staatsblad N.386, 1993 Staatsblad N.49, 1993

P	Decreto-lei N.84/76, 28/01/76 Decreto-lei N.64-A/89, 27/02/89	Diário da República - I Série N 48 27/2/89

S	Lag om anställningsskydd Lag om medbestämmande I arbetslivet Lag om vissa anställningsfrämjande åtgärder	Svensk författningssamling(SFS)1982:80 Svensk författningssamling (SFS) 1976:580 Svensk författningssamling (SFS) 1974:13

UK	Statute Employment Protection Act 1975, 03/02/76 Statute Employment Protection (offshore Employment) Act, 1976 Statute Industrial Relations Act 1976 Industrial Relations Order, 1976 Trade Union Reform and Employment Rights Act 1993	Statutory Rules of Northern Ireland 27/07/76 Statutory Rules of Northern Ireland N.1043, 1976

IMPROVED LIVING AND WORKING CONDITIONS

Transfers of undertakings - Safeguarding of employees' rights

Council Directive 77/187/EEC of 14 February 1977 on the approximation of the laws of the Member States relating to the safeguarding of employees' rights in the event of transfers of undertakings, businesses or parts of businesses.

1) Deadline for implementation of the legislation in the Member States

12.02.1977

2) References

Official Journal L 61, 05.03.1977

A	Arbeitsvertragsrechts-Anpassungsgesetz-Avrag Gesetz vom 01/06/95 zur Änderung der Landarbeitsordnung 1985 Bundesgesetz zur Änderung des Arbeitskräfteüberlassungs- und das Arbeitsverfassungsgesetzes	Bundesgesetzblatt Nr.459/1993, 09/07/93 Landesgesetzblatt für Kärnten N.69/85, 25/08/95 Bundesgesetzblatt N.460/93, 09/07/93

B	Arrêté Royal du/Koninklijk Besluit van 19/04/78, N.8456 Arrêté Royal du/Koninklijk Besluit van 31/10/78, N.8664 Convention collective du 07/06/85 N.32 bis modifiée par la Convention N.32Ter du 02/12/86	Moniteur Belge du/Belgisch Staatsblad van 25/08/78 Moniteur Belge du/Belgisch Staatsblad van 31/10/78 Moniteur Belge /Belgisch Staatsblad

D	Gesetz, 25/08/69 Gesetz, 15/01/72 Gesetz, 13/08/80	Bundesgesetzblatt, (Teile I, II, III) I, N.83, S.1317, 27/08/69 Bundesgesetzblatt, (Teile I, II, III) I, N.2, S.13, 15/01/72 Bundesgesetzblatt, (Teile I, II, III) I, N.48, S.1308, 20/08/80

DK	Lov, 21/03/79	Lovtidende A. N.11, S.326, 21/03/79

E	Ley N.8/80, 10/03/80 Décret N.2065/74, 30/05/74	Boletín Oficial del Estado 14/03/80 Boletín Oficial del Estado 30/07/80

EL	Décret présidentiel N.572, 01/12/88	Journal Officiel, N.269, Volume A, p.4099, 06/12/88

F	Accord Conventionnel Collectif Nat. Retraîte Prévoyance Cadres 14/03/47 Code du Travail (Art. 122-12, 122-12.1, 132-8, 412-16, 412-18) Arrêté Ministériel du 27/03/62 Circulaire N.27/75 du 02/07/75 Accord (Protocole d'Accord) du 01/10/76 Loi N.82-915 Loi N.83-528	Journal Officiel, 29/10/82 Journal Officiel, 29/06/83

FIN	Työsopimuslaki (320/70), 30/04/70, muutos (1354/93), 22/12/93 Laki yhteistoiminnasta yrityksissä (725/78,22/08/78, muutos(236/93), 26/02/93	Suomen Säädöskokoelma 8.3.1993, p 515 Suomen Säädöskokoelma 27.12.1993, p 3563

I	Legge N.675, 12/08/77 Legge N.215, 26/05/78 Codice Civile (Art. 2112), modifié par l'article 47 de la Legge 29/12/90, N.428	Gazzetta Ufficiale N.243, p.6257, 07/09/77 Gazzetta Ufficiale N.145, p.3803, 27/05/78 Gazzetta Ufficiale N.10, p.27, 12/01/91

IRL	European Comunity (Safeguarding of Employees on Transfer of Undertaking) Act	Statutory Instrument N.306 of 1980

L	Règlement Grand Ducal, 19/06/70 Loi, 24/06/70 Règlement Grand Ducal, 27/06/70 Loi, 12/11/71 Loi, 18/03/81	Mémorial A, N.35, 30/06/70 Mémorial A, N.35, 30/06/70 Mémorial A, N.35, 30/06/70 Mémorial A, N.82, 01/12/71 Mémorial A, N.16, 26/03/81

NL	Wet, 15/07/79 Ministeriële Verordening, 30/01/81 Wet, 15/05/81 Wet, 22/05/81	Staatsblad 1979/448, 31/08/79 Staatsblad 1981/18, 05/02/81 Staatsblad 1981/400, 07/07/81 Staatsblad 1981/416, 14/07/81

P	Decreto-lei N.49/408, 24/11/69 Decreto-lei 215-B/75, 30/04/75 Decreto-lei N.519 C/79, 29/12/79 Lei N.46/79, 12/09/79 Lei N.68/79, 09/10/79 Decreto-lei N.64-A/89, 27/02/89	Diário da República, 24/11/69 Diário da República, 30/04/75 Diário da República, 29/12/79 Diário da República, 27/02/89

S	Lag om ändring i lagen om anställningsskydd, 1982:80 Lag om ändring i lagen om medbestämmande i arbetslivet, 1994:1686 Lag om ändring i lagen om arbetstagares rätt till ledighet för utbilding, 1974:981 Lag om ändring i semesterlagen 1977:480 Lag om ändring i lagen vissa anställingsfrämjande åtgarder, 1974:13 Lag om ändring i sekretesslagen, 1980:100 Lag om anställningsskydd Lag om medbestämmande I arbetslivet Semesterlag Lag om äfacklig förtroendemans ställning på arbetsplatsen Lag om ätryggande av pensions utfästelse m.m.	Svensk författningssamling (SFS) 1994:1685 Svensk författningssamling (SFS) 1994:1986 Svensk författningssamling (SFS) 1994:1687 Svensk författningssamling (SFS) 1994:1688 Svensk författningssamling (SFS) 1994:1689 Svensk författningssamling (SFS) 1994:1610 Svensk författningssamling(SFS) 1982:80 Svensk författningssamling (SFS) 1976:580 Svensk författningssamling (SFS) 1977:480 Svensk författningssamling (SFS) 1974:358 Svensk författningssamling (SFS) 1967: 531

UK	Regulations 1981 Trade Union Reform and Employment Rights Act 1993	Statutory Instrument 1981 N.1794

IMPROVED LIVING AND WORKING CONDITIONS

Insolvency of the employer

Council Directive 80/987/EEC of 20 October 1980 on the approximation of the laws of the Member States relating to the protection of employees in the event of the insolvency of their employer.

Council Directive 87/164/EEC of 2 March 1987 amending, on account of the accession of Spain, Directive 80/987/EEC on the approximation of the laws of the Member States relating to the protection of employees in the event of the insolvency of their employer.

1) Deadline for implementation of the legislation in the Member States

Directive 80/987/EEC: 24.10.1983

Directive 87/164/EEC: not required

2) References

Official Journal L 283, 20.10.1980

Official Journal L 66, 11.03.1997

A	Bundesgesetz zur Änderung des Arbeitslosenversicherungs- und des Insolvenzentgeltsicherungsgesetzes	Bundesgesetzblatt N.817/1993, 30/11/93
	Betriebspensionsschutzgesetz N.282/90	Bundesgesetzblatt N.335/1993

B	Loi du/Wet van 28/06/66 Loi du/Wet van 30/06/67	
		Moniteur Belge du/Belgisch Staatsblad van 13/07/67, p.7545
	Arrêté Royal du/Koninklijk Besluit van 06/07/67 pris en exécution de l'article 6 de la loi du 30/06/67	Moniteur Belge du.Belgisch Staatsblad van 13/07/67, p.7547
	Loi du/Wet van 09/07/75 Arrêté Royal du/Koninklijk Besluit van 14/05/85, concernant l'application, aux institutions privées de prévoyance de la loi du 09/07/75 Arrêté Royal du/Koninklijk Besluit van 05/07/85	

D	Arbeitsförderungsgesetz, 25/06/69 § 141a - 141n, § 186b - 186c Gesetz zur Verbesserung der betrieblichen Altersversorgung, 19/12/74 Gesetz, 20/12/82	Bundesgesetzblatt Teil I, S.1857, 23/12/82

DK	Lov om Lønmodtagernes Garantifond, 13/04/72 (i versionen af bekendtgørelsen N.77 af 12/02/88) Lov, 28/04/82 Bekendtgørelse N.172, 28/03/88 Lov N.326 om tilsyn med firmapensionskasser, 24/05/89 Lovbekendtgørelse N.266, 22/04/95 Lov om Forsikingsaktiviteter Lovbekendtgørelse N.511, 16/06/92	Lovtidende N.562, 19/10/82

E	Real Decreto N.2766/67, 16/11/67 Real Decreto N.2123/71, 23/07/71 Estatuto de los trabajadores (Ley N.8/1980, 10/03/80), Art.33 Real Decreto N.505/85, 06/03/85 Orden, 20/08/85 Ley N.11/94, 19/05/94 Real Decreto N.1424/85, 01/08/85 Real Decreto N.1382/85, 01/08/85 Real Decreto N.1683/87, 30/12/87 Ley del 08/05/87	Boletín Oficial del Estado, 14/03/80 Boletín Oficial del Estado, 17/04/85 Boletín Oficial del Estado N.122, p.15805, 23/5/94

EL	Loi N.1414/84 du 30/01/84 Décret Royal de 1964 Loi N.1069/80, 23/08/80, parag.3, art.1	Journal Officiel, Volume A Journal Officiel du 05/07/94

F	Loi N.73-623, 10/07/73 Loi N.73-1194, 27/12/73 Décret N.74-808, 16/09/74 Loi N.75-1251, 27/12/75 Loi N.84-148, 01/03/84 Loi N.85-98, 25/01/85 (redressem.) Loi N.85-99, 25/01/85 (adm. judic. Décret N.85-295, 01/03/85 Décret N.85-388, 27/12/85 Loi N.89-488, 10/07/89 Décret N.86-353, 06/03/86 Articles L.143-11-1 à 143-11-9, Articles D. 143-2 à 143-4 du Code du Travail (dans la version de la Loi N.85-98 du 25/01/85)	

FIN	Palkkaturvalaki (649/73) 10/08/73 Merimiesten palkkaturvalaki (927/79), 21/12/79	

I	Legge N.297, 29/05/82, Art.2 Decreto Legislativo N.80, 27/01/92 Codice civile (Art.2082) Codice commerciale (Art.437) Legge N.95, 03/04/79 Decreto Legislativo N.103,29/03/91	

IRL	Redundancy Payments Act, 1967 Regulations 14 of the Social Welfare (contributions) Regulations of 1979 (S.I. n° 135) Protection of Employees (Employers Insolvency) Act, 30/11/84 Protection of Employees (Employer's Insolvency) (Forms and Procedure) Regulation, 20/12/84 Social Welfare (consolidation) Act of 1993 Protection of Employees (Employer's Insolvency) (Occupational Pension Scheme) (Forms and Procedure) Regulations 1985 Protection of Employees (Employer's Insolvency) (Specification of Date) Regulations 1985	

	Protection of Employees (Employer's Insolvency) (Specification of Date) Regulations 1986 Protection of Employees (Employer's Insolvency) Act 1984 (Amendment Order) 1988 Reduncy Payments Acts 1967 Social Welfare Act 1993	
L	Loi du 30/06/76 portant: 1.Création d'un fonds pour l'emploi; 2. Réglementation de l'octroi des indemnités de chômage complet, telle qu'elle a été modifiée (dans la version du 01/06/87) Loi du 24/05/89, Art. 42, 46 Loi du 08/04/82	Mémorial A, 17/05/82
NL	Wet van 06/11/86, Art. 61-68 Wet van 15/05/52	
P	Decreto-lei N.519 C/79, 29/12/79 Despacho Normativo N.90/85, 02/09/85 Decreto-lei N.28/84, 14/08/84 Decreto-lei N.50/85, 27/02/85 Decreto-lei N.64A/89, 27/02/89 Decreto-lei N.40/86, 14/03/86 Lei N.28/84, 14/08/84	Diário da República, 29/12/79 Diário da República, 14/08/84 Diário da República, 27/02/85 Diário da República N.48, p.862, 27/02/89
S	Lönegarantilag Lönegarantiförordning Förmånsrättslag Lag om allmän försäkring Lag om socialavgifter Konkurslag	Svensk författningssamling 1992:497 Svensk författningssamling 1992:501 Svensk författningssamling 1970:979, ändring SFS 1994:639 Svensk författningssamling 1962:381 Svensk författningssamling 1981:691 Svensk författningssamling 1987:672

UK	Employment Protection (Consolidation) Act 1978 du 31/07/78, articles 122-127, 141, 144-146, 153 European Community Act 1978 C,44 Regulations 1983	Statutory Rules of Northern Ireland N.282, 19/09/83
	Insolvency Act 1986 Reg.39 Social Security Regulation 1979 Income and Corporation Taxes Act 1982 Occupational Pension Schemes (contracting art.)Regulations 1984	

IMPROVED LIVING AND WORKING CONDITIONS

Employer's obligation to inform employees of the conditions applicable to the employment contract or relationship

Council Directive 91/533/EEC of 14 October 1991 on an employer's obligation to inform employees of the conditions applicable to the contract or employment relationship.

1) Deadline for implementation of the legislation in the Member States

30.06.93

2) References

Official Journal L 288, 18.10.91

A	Gesetz vom 1/6/95, mit dem die landarbeitsordnung 1985 geändert wird Arbeitsvertragsrecht-Ampassungsgesetz	Landesgesetzblatt für Kärnten N.69/95, 25/8/95 Bundesgesetzblatt für die Republik Österreich N.459/93
	Arbeits-u. Sozialgerichtsgesetz	Bundesgesetzblatt für die Republik Österreich N.104/85

B	Arrêté Royal du/Koninklijk Besluit van 01/07/94	Moniteur Belge du/Belgisch Staatsblad van 15/07/94, p.18636
	Arrêté Royal du/Koninklijk Besluit van 23/12/94	Moniteur Belge du/Belgisch Staatsblad van 31/12/94, p.32731
	Arrêté Ministériel du/Ministerieel Besluit van 22/12/94	Moniteur Belge du/Belgisch Staatsblad van 06/01/95, p.181

D	Gesetz zur Anpassung arbeitsrechtlicher Bestimmungen an das EG-Recht vom 20/06/95	Bundesgesetzblatt, Jahrgang 1995, Teil I N.38, 20/07/95

DK	Lov N.392, 22/06/93 Bekendtgørelse N.365, 09/06/93 Lov N.1004, 19/12/92	Lovtidende A, 1993 Hæfte N.83

E	Orden 09/02/84	Boletín Oficial del Estado 21/02/84
	Real Decreto N.1989/84, 17/10/84	Boletín Oficial del Estado 09/11/84
	Real Decreto N.1992/84, 31/10/84	Boletín Oficial del Estado 09/11/84
	Real Decreto N.1991/84, 31/10/84	Boletín Oficial del Estado 09/11/84
	Real Decreto N.2104/84, 23/11/84	Boletín Oficial del Estado 23/11/84
	Real Decreto N.1006/85, 26/06/85	Boletín Oficial del Estado 27/06/85
	Real Decreto N.1368/85, 17/07/85	Boletín Oficial del Estado 08/08/85
	Real Decreto N.1382/85, 01/08/85	Boletín Oficial del Estado 12/08/85
	Real Decreto N.1435/85, 01/08/85	Boletín Oficial del Estado 14/08/85
	Real Decreto N.1438/85, 01/08/85	Boletín Oficial del Estado 15/08/85
	Real Decreto N.2/86, 23/05/86	Boletín Oficial del Estado 27/05/86
	Autonomica Ley 8/1988, 07/04/88	
	Real Decreto Legislativo N.521/90, 27/04/90	Boletín Oficial del Estado N.105, 02/05/90
	Articulos 8.2., 8.3 Y 41 del Estatuto de los Trabajadores	
	Real Decreto Comunidad Autonoma Navarra N.2317/93, 29/12/94	Boletín Oficial del Estado N.313, p.37799, 31/12/93
	Ley N.2/91	Boletín Oficial del Estado N.7, 08/01/91
	Ley N.10/94, 19/05/94	Boletín Oficial del Estado N.122, p.15800, 23/5/94
	Ley N.11/94, 19/05/94	Boletín Oficial del Estado N.122, p.15805, 23/5/94
	Ley N.14/94, 01/06/94	Boletín Oficial del Estado N.131, p.17408, 2/6/94

EL	Décret présidentiel N.156 du 02/07/94	Journal Officiel N.102 du 05/07/94, p.1395

F	Décret N.94-760 du 26/08/94 Décret N.94-761 du 31/08/94, portant modification de l'article R 141-10 du code du travail	Journal Officiel du 02/09/94, p.12731 Journal Officiel du 02/09/94, p.12731

FIN	Työsopimuslaki 70/320, muutos 93/1354	

I	Decreto-legge del 01/10/1996 n.511 Legge del 18/01/72 n.1204	Gazzetta Ufficiale - Serie generale del 02/10/1996 N.231 p.23 Gazzetta Ufficiale - Serie generale N.14

IRL	Terms of Employment (Information) Act 1993 (N.58 of 1993)	Statutory Instrument N.96 of 1993

L	Loi du 15/05/95, modifiant la loi du 24/05/89 sur le contrat de travail et la loi du 23/07/93 portant diverses mesures en faveur de l'emploi	Mémorial A, N. 43,29/05/95

NL	Wet van 02/12/93 tot uitvoering van Richtlijn van Raad van Europese Gemeenschappen betreffende Informatie van Werknemer over zijn Arbeidsovereenkomst of Arbeidsverhouding	Staatsblad 1993, N.635

P	Decreto-lei N.5/94, 11/01/94	Diário da República I Serie A N.8, p.100, 11/1/94

S	Lag om anställningsskydd	Svensk författningssamling (SFS) 1982:80

UK	Trade Union Reform and Employment Rights Act 1993	

INFORMATION, CONSULTATION AND PARTICIPATION OF WORKERS

European Works Council or procedure for information

Council Directive 94/45/EC of 22 September 1994 on the establishment of a European Works Council or a procedure in Community-scale undertakings and Community-scale groups of undertakings for the purposes of informing and consulting employees.

1) Deadline for implementation of the legislation in the Member States

22.09.96

2) References

Official Journal L 254, 30.09.94

A	Bundesgesetz, mit dem das Arbeitsverfassungsgesetz, das Arbeits- und Sozialgerichtsgesetzes und das Bundesgesetz über die Post-Betriebsverfassung geândert werden	Bundesgesetzblatt fûr die Republik Österreich Nr 601/96, 31/10/96

B	Arrêté Royal du/Koninklijk Besluit van 22/03/96	Moniteur Belge du/Belgisch Staatsblad van 11/04/96, p.8465

D	Gesetz über Europäische Betriebsräte (EBRG) vom 28/10/96	Bundesgesetzblatt Teil I vom 31/10/96, S.1548

DK	Lov N.371 af 22/05/96 om europæiske samarbejdsudvalg	Ministerialtidende , j.nr.1995-534-8

E	Ley sobre derechos de información y consulta de los trabajadorcs cnlas empresas y grupos de empresas de dimensión comunitaria N 10/97 : 24/4/97	Boletín oficial del Estado N 99, 25/4/97 p 13258

EL	Décret présidentiel n° 40/97, 18/3/97	FEK A n° 39 20/3/97 p 599

F	Loi N.96-985 du 12/11/95	Journal Officiel du 13/11/96

FIN	Laki yhteistoiminnasta yrityksissä annetun lain muuttamisesta 614/96, 9/8/96	

I	Accordo Interconfederale per il Recepimento della direttiva 94/45, 06/11/96	

IRL	Transnational Information and Consultation of Employees Act of 1996 Transnational Information and Consultation of Employees Act of 1996 (Commencement) Order of 1996	Statutory Instruments N.20 of 1996 Statutory Instruments N.276 of 1996

L		

NL	Wet van 23/1/97 tot uitvoering van richtlijn 94/45/EG	Staatsblad 1997/32 pp1-13 4/2/97

P		

S	Lag om europeiska företagsråd	Svensk författningssamling (SFS) 1996:359

UK	Not yet applicable	

IMPROVED LIVING AND WORKING CONDITIONS

Posting of workers

Directive 96/71/EC of the European Parliament and of the Council of 16 December 1996 concerning the posting of workers in the framework of the provision of services.

1) Deadline for implementation of the legislation in the Member States

16.12.1999

2) References

Official Journal L 18, 21.01.1997

A		
B		
D		
DK		

E		
EL		
F		
FIN		
I		
IRL		
L		
NL		

P		
S		
UK		

EQUAL TREATMENT FOR MEN AND WOMEN

Equal pay principle

Council Directive 75/117/EEC of 10 February 1975 on the approximation of the laws of the Member States relating to the application of the principle of equal pay for men and women.

1) Deadline for implementation of the legislation in the Member States

12.02.1976

2) References

Official Journal L 45, 19.02.75

A	Landarbeitsverordnung	Landesgesetzblatt für Niederösterreich N.9020/15
	Gesetz zur Änderung des Wiener land- u. forstwirtschaftlichen Gleichbehandlungsgesetz	Landesgesetzblatt für Wien N.7/94, 14/02/94
	Landes-Gleichbehandlungsgesetz-LGBG	Landesgesetzblatt für Salzburg N.30/96 19/03/96
	Wiener-Gleichbehandlungsgesetz	Landesgesetzblatt für Wien N.18/96, 18/04/96
	Bediensteten-Schutzgesetz	Landesgesetzblatt für Niederösterreich N.2015-1
	Dienstpragmatik der Landesbeamten DPL	Landesgesetzblatt für Niederösterreich N.2200-33
	Landesbeamtendienstordnung 1976 (GBDO)	Landesgesetzblatt für Niederösterreich N.2400-19
	Gemeinde-Vertragsbedienstetengesetz (GVBG)	Landesgesetzblatt für Niederösterreich N.2420-24
	Act on Equality Treatment	Landesgesetzblatt für Kärnten, N.56/94
	Bundesgesetz zur Änderung des Beamten-Dienstrechtsgesetz 1997, das Gehaltsgesetz 1956, des Vertragsbedienstetengesetz 1948, des Pensionsgesetz 1965, des Bundeslehrer-Lehrverpflichtungsgesetz, des Landeslehrer-Dienstrechtsgesetz 1984, des Land- und forstwirtschaftliche Landeslehrer- Dienstrechtgesetz 1985, des Bundes-Personalvertretungsgesetz, der Bundesforste-Dienstordnung 1986, des Bundsgleichbehandlungsgesetz, des Ausschreibungsgesetz 1989, des Dienstrechtsverfahrensgesetz 1984, des Auslandseinsatzzulagengesetz, des Nebengebührenzulagengesetz, des Bezügegesetz, des Richterdienstgesetz und des Karenzurlaubsgesetz	Bundesgesetzblatt N.16/1994, 05/01/94

	Gleichbehandlungsgesetz (GBG)	Bundesgesetzblatt N.108/79, 833/92
	Kundmachung des Bundeskanzlers vom 09/12/80, über die Berichtigung von Druckfehlern im Bundesgesetzblatt und in der amtlichen Sammlung wiederverlautbarer österr. Rechtsvorschriften	Bundesgesetzblatt N.577/80, 23/12/80
	Bundesgleichbehandlungsgesetz	Bundesgesetzblatt N.100/93, 12/02/93

B	Arrêté Royal du/Koninklijk Besluit van 24/10/67	Moniteur Belge/Belgisch Staatsblad
	Loi du/Wet van 16/03/71	Moniteur Belge/Belgisch Staatsblad
	Arrêté Royal du/Koninklijk Besluit van 09/12/75	Moniteur Belge/Belgisch Staatsblad
	Loi du/Wet van 04/08/78 (titre V/Titel V) (Equal Treatment)	Moniteur Belge du/Belgisch Staatsblad van 17/08/78

D	Gesetz, 23/05/49	Bundesgesetzblatt
	Gesetz, 05/01/72	Bundesgesetzblatt
	Gesetz, 15/03/74	Bundesgesetzblatt
	Gesetz, 13/08/80	Bundesgesetzblatt

DK	Centralt forlig mellem arbejdsgierorganisationen og arbejdstager 31/10/73 (ændr. 1981)	31/10/73
	Lov af 04/02/76	
	Lov af 19/02/86	
	Lov af 01/01/88	

E	Ley N.39/62, 21/07/62	Boletin Oficial del Estado, 23/07/62
	Convenio III O.I.T., 26/10/67	Boletin Oficial del Estado, 04/12/68
	Ley Organica N.2/79, 03/10/79	Boletin Oficial del Estado, 05/10/79
	Ley 8/80 de 10/03/80	Boletin Oficial del Estado, 14/03/80
	Real Decreto Legislativo N.1568/80 13/06/80	Boletin Oficial del Estado, 30/06/80
	DR N.2347/85, 04/12/85	
	Constitution, 27/12/87	Boletin Oficial del Estado, 29/12/87
	Ley N.3/89, 03/03/89	
	Articulo 28 del Código del Trabajo	

EL	Constitution Art. 22	Journal Officiel
	Loi N.754, 1978	
	Loi N.1041, 1980	
	Loi N.1414, 1984, 30/01/84	Journal Officiel N.10, Volume A, 02/02/84

F	Loi du 22/12/72 Décret, 27/03/73 Loi N.83-635, 13/07/83	Journal Officiel Journal Officiel Journal Officiel

FIN	Laki naisten ja miesten välisestätsa-arvosta (609/86), 08/08/86, muutos (624/92), 08/07/92	

I	Legge N.604, 15/07/66 Legge N.300, 20/05/70 Legge N.903, 09/12/77	Gazzetta Ufficiale, 06/08/66 Gazzetta Ufficiale, 27/05/70 Gazzetta Ufficiale, 18/12/77

IRL	Acts of Oireachts, 01/07/74 Acts of Oireachts, 01/06/77	

L	Loi, 22/06/63 Arrêté Grand Ducal 22/04/63 Loi du 12/06/65 Loi du 12/03/73 Règl. Grand Ducal, 10/07/74 Loi du 08/12/81	

NL	Wet 27/12/68 Koninklijk Besluit, 29/11/73 Wet 20/03/75 Wet 02/07/80 Wet 01/03/80	 Staatsblad 1975 Staatsblad 1980 Staatsblad 1980

P	Decreto-lei N.392-79, 20/09/79 Decreto-lei N.426-88 Decreto-lei N.5/94	Diário da Republica, 20/09/79 Diário da Republica, 18/11/88

S	Jämställdhetslag Förordning med instruktion för jämställdhetsombudsmannen	Svensk förmattningssamling 1991:433 Svensk förmattningssamling 1991:1438

UK	Statute Equal Pay Act, 29/05/70 Statute Equal Pay Act 1970 Equal Pay Ordinance Gibraltar, 24/10/75 Statute Sex Discrimination Act, 12/11/75 Equal Pay Regulations 1983 Statute Sex Discrimination Act, 07/11/86 Turera 1993	Statutory Rules of Northern Ireland 1970 Statutory Instrument, 1983

EQUAL TREATMENT FOR MEN AND WOMEN

Access to employment, vocational training and promotion

Council Directive 76/207/EEC of 9 February 1976 on the implementation of the principle of equal treatment for men and women as regards access to employment, vocational training and promotion, and working conditions.

1) Deadline for implementation of the legislation in the Member States

12.08.1978

2) References

Official Journal L 39, 14.02.1976

A	Burgenländisches Feuerwehrgesetz Bgld.FWG 1994, 26/05/94	Landesgesetzblatt für das Burgenland N.49/1994
	Gesetz zur Änderung des Wiener land- u. forstwirtschaftlichen Gleichbehandlungsgesetz	Landesgesetzblatt für Wien N.7/94, 14/02/94
	Bundesgleichbehandlungsgesetz-G- GBG	Bundesgesetzblatt N.100/1993, idF.BGBl N.16/1994
	Gleichbehandlungsgesetz	Bundesgesetzblatt N.108/1979, idF.BGBl N.833/1992
	Arbeitsmarktförderungsgesetz (AMFG)	Bundesgesetzblatt 31/69, zuletzt geändert durch BGBl. N.25/1994
	Änderung des Akademie-Organisationsgesetz	Bundesgesetzblatt N.105/1993
	Änderung des KunsthochschulOrganisationsgesetz	Bundesgesetzblatt N.104/1993
	Landesarbeitsordnung	Landesgesetzblatt für Niederösterreich N.9020-15
	Landes-Gleichbehandlungsgesetz L-GBG	Landesgesetzblatt für Salzburg N.30/96 19/03/96
	Wiener-Gleichbehandlungsgesetz	Landesgesetzblatt für Wien N.18/96, 18/04/96
	Act on Equality Treatment	Landesgesetzblatt für Kärnten, N.56/94
	Gemeinde-Vertragsbedienstetengesetz (GVBG)	Landesgesetzblatt für Niederösterreich N.2420-24
	Bediensteten-Schutzgesetz	Landesgesetzblatt für Niederösterreich N.2015-1
	Dienstpragmatik der Landesbeamten DPL	Landesgesetzblatt für Niederösterreich N.2200-33
	Gemeindebeamtendienstordnung 1976 (GBDO)	Landesgesetzblatt für Niederösterreich N.2400-19
	Convention on the Elimination of all Forms of Discrimination against Woman	Bundesgesetzblatt N.443/1982

B	Loi du/Wet van 04/08/78	Moniteur Belge du/Belgisch Staatsblad van 17/08/78
	Arrêté Royal du/Koninklijk Besluit van 05/10/88	Moniteur Belge du/Belgisch Staatsblad van 18/11/88, p.15958
	Loi du/Wet van 20/07/90	Moniteur Belge du/Belgisch Staatsblad van 15/08/90, p.15875

D	Gesetz 13/08/80 (Arbeitsrechtliches EG-Anpassungsgesetz)	Bundesgesetzblatt (Teile I, II, III) I S.1308, 13/08/80

DK	Lov N.161, 12/04/78	Lovtidende A, p.490, 1978
	Lov N.162, 12/04/78	Lovtidende A, p.492, 1978

E	Ley N.31/62, 21/07/62	Boletín Oficial del Estado, 23/07/62
	Ley Organica N.2/79, 03/10/79	Boletín Oficial del Estado, 05/10/79
	Ley N.8/80, 10/03/80	Boletín Oficial del Estado, 14/03/80
	Real Decreto Legislativo N.1568/80	Boletín Oficial del Estado, 30/06/80
	Ley N.51/80, 08/10/80	Boletín Oficial del Estado, 17/10/80
	Ley N.31/84, 02/08/84	Boletín Oficial del Estado, 04/08/84

EL	Loi N.1414/84 du 30/01/84	Journal Officiel, Volume A
	Décret Royal du 1964	

F	Loi N.75-625, 11/07/75	Journal Officiel, 13/07/75
	Loi N.89-488, 10/07/89	

FIN	Laki naisten ja miesten välisestätsa-arvosta (609/86), 08/08/86	

I	Legge N.903, 09/12/77 Legge N.125, 10/04/91 Legge N.236, 1993	Gazzetta Ufficiale N.348, 18/12/77

IRL	Acts of Oireachts Employment Equality Act 01/06/77 Act 1993 (Amendment) Abusive Dismissal	Irof N.16, 01/06/77

L	Loi du 08/12/81 (EgalitéTraitement entre homme et femmes) Loi du 17/11/86	Mémorial avis N.91, 16/12/81 Mémorial avis N.93, p.2222, 05/12/86

NL	Wet, 01/03/80 Wet, 02/07/80 Wet (generale sur egalité de traitement)	Staatsblad N.1980/86, 13/03/80 Staatsblad N.1980/384, 02/07/80

P	Decreto-lei N.392/79, 20/09/79 Decreto-lei N.426/88, 18/11/88	Diário da República I, 20/09/79 Diário da República I, 18/11/88

S	Jämställdhetslag Lag om ändring i jämställdhetslagen (1991:433) Förordning med instruktion förjämställdhetsombudsmannen	Svensk förmattningssamling 1991:433 Svensk förmattningssamling 1994:292 Svensk förmattningssamling 1991:1438

UK	Statute Sex Discrimination Act, 1975 (CH.65) Sex Discrimination, Order 1976 Operations at Unfenced Machinery (Amendment) Regulations, 1976 Order 1993 (Regulations (and Appeals) for sex Discrimination and Wages Equality	12/11/75 Statutory Rules of Northern Ireland N.1042, 02/07/76 Statutory Instrument 1976 Statutory Instrument

EQUAL TREATMENT FOR MEN AND WOMEN

Social security

Council Directive 79/7/EEC of 19 December 1978 on the progressive implementation of the principle of equal treatment for men and women in matters of social security.

1) Deadline for implementation of the legislation in the Member States

23.12.1984

2) References

Official Journal L 6, 10.01.1979

A	Pensionsgesetz	Bundesgesetzblatt N.340/1965
	Nebengebührenzulagengesetz	Bundesgesetzblatt N.485/1971
	Bundestheater-Pensionsgesetz	Bundesgesetzblatt N.159/1958
	Bundesforste-Dienstordnung:	Bundesgesetzblatt N.298/1986
	Bundesflegegeldgesetz	Bundesgesetzblatt N.110/1993
	Arbeitslosenversicherungsgesetz	Bundesgesetzblatt N.184/1949
	Sonderunterstützungsgesetz	Bundesgesetzblatt N.642/1973
	Überbrückungshilfengesetz	Bundesgesetzblatt N.174/1963
	Allgemeines Sozialversicherungsgesetz (ASVG)	Bundesgesetzblatt N.189/1955
	Gewerbliches Sozialversicherungsgesetz (GSVG)	Bundesgesetzblatt N.560/1978
	Bauern-Sozialversicherungsgesetz (BSVG)	Bundesgesetzblatt N.559/1978
	Beamten-Kranken und Unfallversicherungsgesetz (B-KUVG)	Bundesgesetzblatt N.200/1967
	Notarversicherungsgesetz NVG 1972	Bundesgesetzblatt N.66/1972
	Freiberufliches Sozialversicherungsgesetz (FSVG)	Bundesgesetzblatt N.624/1978
	Entgeltfortzahlungsgesetz (EFZG)	Bundesgesetzblatt N.399/1974
	Nachtswerarbeitsgesetz (NSchG)	Bundesgesetzblatt N.473/1992
	Bundesverfassungsgesetz über unterschiedliche Altersgrenzen von männlichen und weiblichen Sozialversicherten	Bundesgesetzblatt N.832/1992
	Arbeitsrechtliches Begleitgesetz - ArbBG	Bundesgesetzblatt N.833/1992
	Sozialrechtstandgesetz	Bundesgesetzblatt N.335/1993
	Sozialrechtstandgesetz	Bundesgesetzblatt N.336/1993
	Novelle Bauern Sozialrecht	Bundesgesetzblatt N. 337/1993
	Pflegegeldgesetz 1993 (NOE PGG)	Landesrechtssammlung für Niederösterreich N.9220-0 LGBl. 47/1993 (Stammgesetz)idF der

NOE Sozialhilfegesetz - NOE SHG	1.Novelle Landesrechtssammlung für Niederösterreich N.9220-1 LGBl. 122/1995 Landesrechtssammlung für Niederösterreich, N. 9200-0 LGBl. 78/1974
Gemeindebeamtendienstordnung 1976	Landesrechtssammlung für Niederösterreich N.2400-0 LGBl. 111/1976
Dienstpragmatik der Landesbeamten	Landesrechtssammlung für Niederösterreich, N. 2200-0 LGBl. 93/1972
Gesetz vom 06/08/73 über die Sozialhilfe	Landesgesetzblatt für Oberösterreich N.66/1973
Behindertengesetz, 03/07/91	Landesgesetzblatt für Oberösterreich N.113/1991
Pflegegeldgesetz - O.oe. PGG, 02/06/93	Landesgesetzblatt für Oberösterreich N.64/1993
Landesbeamtengesetz - O.oe. LBG, 03/03/1993	Landesgesetzblatt für Oberösterreich N. 65/1995
Landes-Vertragsbedienstetengesetz-O.oe. LVBG, 03/03/93	Landesgesetzblatt für Oberösterreich N. 10/1994
Gemeindebedienstetengesetz 1982	Landesgesetzblatt für Oberösterreich N. 1/1982
Statutargemeinden-Beamtengesetz, 31/08/56	Landesgesetzblatt für Oberösterreich N.37/1956
Satzung der Krankenfürsorge für o.oe. Landesbeamte: Beschluss der o.oe. Landesregierung vom 05/08/85	
Gesetz vom 08/07/77 über die O.oe. Lehrer-Kranken- und Unfallfürsorge (O.oe. LKUFG)	Landesgesetzblatt für Oberösterreich N.66/1983
Gemeinde-Unfallfuersorgegesetz 09/05/69	Landesgesetzblatt für Oberösterreich N.36/1969
Landesbeamten-Pensionsgesetz	Landesgesetzblatt für Oberösterreich N. 22/1966
Nebengebührenzulagengesetz 17/07/1973	Landesgesetzblatt für Oberösterreich N.60/1973
Steiermärkisches Sozialhilfegesetz 09/11/76	Landesgesetzblatt der Steiermark N. 1/1977
Steiermärkisches Pflegegeldgesetz StPGG, 15/06/1993	Landesgesetzblatt der Steiermark N. 80/1993
Landesbeamtengesetz 1994	Landesgesetzblatt für Tirol, N.19/1994
Gemeindebeamtengesetz 1970	Landesgesetzblatt für Tirol, N.44/1970
Tiroler Sozialhilfegesetz 23/10/1973	Landesgesetzblatt für Tirol,N.105/1973
Tiroler Pflegegeldgesetz, 24/06/93	Landesgesetzblatt für Tirol, N.55/1993
Gemeindebedienstetengesetz-GBedG.	Landesgesetzblatt für Voralberg, N.49/1988
Landes-Pflegegeldgesetz, L-PGG	Landesgesetzblatt für Vorarlberg, N. 38/1993
Behindertengesetz	Landesgesetzblatt für Vorarlberg, N. 9/1994
Sozialhilfegesetz - SHG.	Landesgesetzblatt für Vorarlberg, N. 26/1971
Landesbedienstetengesetz - LBedG.	Landesgesetzblatt für Vorarlberg, N. 1/1988
Kärntner Pflegegeldgesetz,14/06/93	Landesgesetzblatt für Kärnten, N.76/93
Kärntner Sozialhilfegesetz 1981	Landesgesetzblatt für Kärnten, N.30/81
Kärntner Dienstrechtgesetzes	Landesgesetzblatt für Kärnten, N.71/94
Gemeindebedienstetensgesetz 1992	Landesgesetzblatt für Kärnten, N.56/92
Stadtbeamtengesetz 1993	Landesgesetzblatt für Kärnten, N.115/1993
Gemeindebedienstetengesetz 1971	Landesgesetzblatt für das Burgenland N. 13/1972 und LGBl. N. 25/1972 (DFB), idF LGBl. N. 25/1980, 43/1989 u. 51/91
Burgenländisches Sozialhilfegesetz 13/11/74	Landesgesetzblatt für das Burgenland N. 7/1975 idF LGBl. N. 38/1975 (DBF)
Landesbeamtengesetz 1985	Landesgesetzblatt für das Burgenland N. 48/1985, samt Novellen idF LGBl. N. 60/1995

	Burgenländisches Behindertengesetz 03/05/66	Landesgesetzblatt für das Burgenland N.20/1966 idF LGBl. N. 2/1995
	Burgenländisches Pflegegeldgesetz 17/06/93	Landesgesetzblatt für das Burgenland N.58/1993, 01/07/93
	Gesetz ueber die Regelung der Sozialhilfe (WSHG)	Landesgesetzblatt für Wien, N. 11/1973 26/03/73
	1. Sozialhilfegesetznovelle	Landesgesetzblatt fuer Wien N.38/1975 29/12/75
	3. Sozialhilfegesetznovelle	Landesgesetzblatt fuer Wien N.17/1986 08/04/86
	5. Sozialhilfegesetznovelle	Landesgesetzblatt fuer Wien N.50/1993 22/09/93
	Bundespflegegesetz	Bundesgesetzblatt N.110/1993

B	Arrêté Royal du/Koninklijk Besluit van 30/07/86	Moniteur Belge du/Belgisch Staatsblad van 02/08/86, p.10854
	Arrêté Royal du/Koninklijk Besluit van 08/08/86	Moniteur Belge du/Belgisch Staatsblad van 27/08/86, p.11825

D	Gesetz, 11/07/85, Article 1	Bundesgesetzblatt Teil I, S.1450, 1985

DK	Lov N.543, 06/10/82 Lov N.249, 08/06/83 Lov N.358, 25/07/83 Lov N.436, 09/09/84 Lov N.217, 16/05/84 Lov N.554, 21/11/93	

E	Decret, 22/06/56 Orden, 05/04/74 Decret N.2065/74 Constitution, 27/12/78 (Art. 14) Real Decreto Legislativo N.1568/80, 13/06/80 Real Decreto N.2620, 24/07/81 Ley N.31/48, 02/08/84 Real Decreto N.625/85, 02/04/85 Ley N.26/85, 31/07/85 Orden, 11/05/88	Boletin Oficial del Estado, 15/07/56 Boletin Oficial del Estado, 30/07/74 Boletin Oficial del Estado, 29/12/78 Boletín Oficial del Estado, 30/06/80 Boletin Oficial Del Estado, 06/11/81 Boletin Oficial Del Estado, 04/08/84 Boletin Oficial Del Estado, 07/05/85 Boletin Oficial Del Estado, 01/08/85

EL	Article 17, Loi N.997/79 Décret présidentiel N.1362/81, Article 4 et 116, Constitution 75 Loi N.1483/84 Loi N.2084/92	

F	Loi N.77/765, 12/07/77 Loi N.77/1466, 30/12/77	

FIN	Laki naisten ja miesten välisestätsa-arvosta (609/86), 08/08/86 Sairausvakuutuslaki (364/63), 04/07/63 Kansaneläkelaki (347/56), 08/06/56 Työntekijän eläkelaki (395/61), 08/07/61 Tapaturmavakuutuslaki (608/48), 20/08/48 Sosiaalihuoltolaki (710/82), 17/09/82 Työttömyysturvalaki (602/84), 24/08/84	

I	Loi N.903/77, 09/12/77	

IRL	Social Welfare (N.2), Act, 1985 (Section 6) (Commencement) Order Social Welfare (N.2) Act, 1985 (Commencement) Order, 1986,	Statutory Instrument, N.173 of 1986 Statutory Instrument, N.365 of 1986

L	Loi, 15/12/86	Mémorial A. N.101, p.2343, 22/12/86

NL	Koninklijk Besluit Ministeriële Beschikking	Staatsblad N.708, 1979 Staatscourant N.214, 1984

34

P	Decret N.45256, 23/09/63	
	Decreto-lei N.160/80, 29/05/80	Diário da República, 29/05/80
	Decreto-lei N.464/80, 13/10/80	Diário da República, 13/10/80
	Portaria N.642/83, 01/06/83	
	Decreto-lei N.26/77, 04/05/77	Diário da República, 04/05/77
	Decreto-lei N.329, 25/09/94	Diário da República, 25/09/94

S	Lag om allmän försäkring	Svensk förmattningssamling 1962:381
	Lag om arbetsskadeförsäkring	Svensk förmattningssamling 1976:380
	Lag om arbetslöshetsförsäkring	Svensk förmattningssamling 1973:370

UK	Social Security Act 1980	
	Social Insurance and Amendment and Benefits 1984	
	Health and Social Security Act, 1984	
	Social Security Regulations 1984 (Server disablement allowances)	

EQUAL TREATMENT FOR MEN AND WOMEN

Occupational social security schemes

Council Directive 86/378/EEC of 24 July 1986 on the implementation of the principle of equal treatment for men and women in occupational social security schemes.

Council Directive 96/97/EC of 20 December 1996 amending Directive 86/378/EEC on the implementation of the principle of equal treatment for men and women in occupational social security schemes.

1) Deadline for implementation of the legislation in the Member States

Directive 86/378/EEC: 31.07.1989

Directive 96/97/EC: 01.07.1997

2) References

Official Journal L 225, 12.08.1986

Official Journal L 46, 17.02.1997

A	Landarbeitsordnung	Landesgesetzblatt für Niederösterreich N.9020-15
	Gesetz zur Änderung des Wiener land- und forstwirtschaftlichen Gleichbehandlungsgesetzes	Landesgesetzblatt für Wien, N.7/1994, 14/02/94
	Landes-Gleichbehandlungsgesetz L-GBG, 14/12/95	Landesgesetzblatt für Salzburg,N.30/96 19/03/96
	Gemeinde-Vertragsbedienstetengesetz (GCBG)	Landesgesetzblatt für Niederösterreich N.2420-4
	Bediensteten-Schutzgesetz	Landesgesetzblatt für Niederösterreich N.2015-1
	DPL (Dienstpragmatik der Landesbeamten)	Landesgesetzblatt für Niederösterreich N.2020-33
	Gemeindebeamtendienstordnung 1976 (GBDO)	Landesgesetzblatt für Niederösterreich N.2400-19
	Gleichbehandlungsgesetz, 23/02/79	Bundesgesetzblatt N.108/79
	Notifizierung von Umsetzungsmaßnahmen 17/4/97	Bundesgesetzblatt p.224-234

B		

D	S.G.V.B. Art. 45 (Code Social) B.G.B. Art. 616 (Code Civil) Gesetz, 19/12/74 Gesetz, 13/10/83 Gesetz, B. Enz. G.G. N.40, S.1551, 05/08/89	Bundesgesetzblatt (Teile I) S.3610 Bundesgesetzblatt (Teile I) S.1261

DK		

E	Constitution Art. 14 Ley N.8/1980, 10/03/80 Ley N.33/84, 02/08/84 Real Decreto N.2615/85, 04/12/85 Real Decreto N.1307/88, 30/09/88 Ley N.8/1990, 28/06/90	Boletín Oficial del Estado N.311, 29/12/78 Boletín Oficial del Estado, 14/03/80 Boletín Oficial del Estado N.186, 04/08/84 Boletín Oficial del Estado N.13, 15/01/86 Boletín Oficial del Estado N.263, 02/11/88 Boletín Oficial del Estado N.194, 14/08/90

EL	Loi N.1876/1990	

F	Loi N.89-474, 10/07/89 Loi N.731-2-1 du Code du Travail	

FIN	Laki naisten ja miesten välisestä tasa-arvosta (609/86)	

I	Legge N.903, 9/12/1977 Legge N.125, 10/4/1991	Gazzetta Ufficiale N.343, p.9041 Gazzetta Ufficiale N.88, 15/4/1991

IRL	Pensions Act 1990 Part VII Statutory Instrument 366 of 1992 Statutory Instrument 286 of 1997, 25/6/97	
L		
NL		
P	Decreto-lei N.396/86, 23/10/86 Decreto-lei N.307/97, 11/11/97	Diário da República I N.272, p.3540, 25/11/86
S	Jämställdhetslag	Svensk författningssamling 1991:433
UK	Social Security Act, 1989 Social Security (N.I.) Order 1989 Equal Treatment section of the Pensions Act 1995 and subsequent Regulations, 7/12/95	The Law relating to Social security, supplements N.38-39, pp.5.1915-1918 and 5.6102-6108

EQUAL TREATMENT FOR MEN AND WOMEN

Self-employed activity, including agricultural work

Council Directive 86/613/EEC of 11 December 1986 on the application of the principle of equal treatment between men and women engaged in an activity, including agriculture, in a self-employed capacity and in the protection of self-employed women during pregnancy and motherhood.

1) Deadline for implementation of the legislation in the Member States

30.06.1989

2) References

Official Journal L 359, 19.12.1986

A	Landarbeitsordnung	Landesgesetzblatt für Niederösterreich N.9020-15
	Gemeinde-Vertragsbedienstetengesetz (GVBG)	Landesgesetzblatt für Niederösterreich N.2420-24
	Bedienstetenschutzgesetz	Landesgesetzblatt für Niederösterreich N.2015-1
	DPL (Dienstpragmatik der Landesbeamten)	Landesgesetzblatt für Niederösterreich N.2200-33
	Gemeindebeamtendienstordnung 1976 (GBDO)	Landesgesetzblatt für Niederösterreich N.2400-19
	Allgemeines Sozialversicherungsgesetz (ASVG)	Bundesgesetzblatt N.189/55
	Gewerbliches Sozialversicherungsgesetz (GSVG)	Bundesgesetzblatt N.560/78
	Bauern- und Sozialversicherungsgesetz (BSVG)	Bundesgesetzblatt N.559/78

B	Arrêté Royal du/Koninklijk Besluit van 20/12/63	Moniteur Belge du/Belgisch Staatsblad van 18/01/64
	Arrêté Royal du/Koninklijk Besluit van 27/07/67, N.38	Moniteur Belge du/Belgisch Staatsblad van 29/07/67
	Loi du/Wet van 04/08/78	
	Loi du/Wet van 14/12/89	

D	Bekanntmachung, 15/03/90	Bundesgesetzblatt N.52, p.1269

DK	Lov N.244, 19/04/89 Lov N.198, 29/03/89 Lov N.686, 11/10/90 Lov, 16/03/89	

E	Ley N.15/67, 08/04/67 Real Decreto N.2530/1970, 20/08/70 Real Decreto N.2530/1970, 20/08/70 Real Decreto N.2123/1971, 23/07/71 Ley N.1/73, 01/03/73 Real Decreto N.2864/1974 Real Decreto N.2864/1974, 30/08/74 Art. 14 Ley Autonomica Ley N.11/81, 13/05/81 Decreto Legislativo 1/84, 19/07/84 Ley N.33/84, 02/08/84 Ley N.3/87, 08/04/87 Ley N.8/1990, 28/06/90	Boletín Oficial del Estado N.86, 11/04/67 Boletín Oficial del Estado N.221, 15/09/71 Boletín Oficial del Estado N.234-13 Boletín Oficial del Estado N.226, 21/09/71 Boletín Oficial del Estado N.63, 14/03/73 Boletín Oficial del Estado N.243, 10/10/74 Boletín Oficial del Estado N.18, 18/11/74 Boletín Oficial del Estado N.311, 29/12/78 Boletín Oficial del Estado N.118, 18/05/81 Boletín Oficial del Estado N.456, 27/07/84 Boletín Oficial del Estado N.186, 04/08/84 Boletín Oficial del Estado N.84, 08/04/87

EL	Loi N. 1287/82	

F	Loi N.85-596, 10/07/82 Décret N.82-1247, 31/12/82 Loi N.85-697, 11/07/85 Décret N.86-100, 04/03/86 Loi N.87-588, 30/07/87 Loi N.89-474, 10/07/89 Décret N.89-628, 24/07/89 Loi N.89-1008, 31/12/89 5ème Code Sécurité Social, Art. Loi N.742-6 Loi N.62-1971, 08/08/62	Journal Officiel Journal Officiel 15/01/83, p.350 Journal Officiel Journal Officiel Journal Officiel Journal Officiel Journal Officiel Journal Officiel Journal Officiel Journal Officiel

FIN	Osakeyhtiölaki (734/78), 29/09/78 Osuuskuntalaki (247/54), 28/05/54 Laki avoimesta yhtiöstä ja kommandiittiyhtiöstä (389/88),29/04/88 Yhdistyslaki (503/89), 26/05/89 Säätiölaki (109/30), 05/04/30 Laki naisten ja miesten välisestätsa-arvosta (609/86), 08/08/86	

I	Constituzione Art. 3, 37 et 51 Legge N.1047, 26/10/57 Legge N.463, 04/07/59 Legge N.66, 09/02/63 Legge N.613, 22/07/66 Legge N.1204, 30/12/71 Legge N.151, 19/05/75 Legge N.903, 09/12/77 Legge N.44, 28/02/86 Legge N.546, 29/12/87 Legge N.379, 11/12/90	 Gazzetta Ufficiale N.278, 11/11/57 Gazzetta Ufficiale N.165, 13/07/59 Gazzetta Ufficiale N.48, 19/02/63 Gazzetta Ufficiale N.200, 12/08/66 Gazzetta Ufficiale N.165, 13/01/72 Gazzetta Ufficiale N.135, 23/05/75 Gazzetta Ufficiale Gazzetta Ufficiale N.50, 01/03/86 Gazzetta Ufficiale, 07/01/88

IRL	Companies Act. 1963 To 1990 (C.4) Unit Trust Act. 1966 (C.5) Credit Union Act. 1966 Social Welfare Act (Consolidation) Act. 1981 (C.6) Social Welfare Act. 1982 Social Welfare Act. 1988	

L	Loi du 30/04/80 Loi du 15/12/86 Règlement Grand-Ducal du 15/12/86 Loi du 01/08/88 Loi du 27/07/92	Memorial A Memorial A Memorial A Memorial A

NL	Wet van 01/03/80 Wet van 01/07/89	Staatsblad 1980, 86 Staatsblad 1989, 68

P	Decreto-lei N.8/82, 18/01/82	Diário da República I, 18/01/82
	Decreto-lei N.401/86, 02/12/86	Diário da República I, 02/12/86
	Decreto Regulamentar N. 75/86, 30/12/86	Diário da República I, 02/12/86
	Decreto-lei N.40/89, 01/02/89	Diário da República I, 01/02/89
	Decreto-lei N.225/89, 06/07/89	
	Decreto-lei N.248/86, 25/08/86	
	Decreto-lei N.307/86, 22/09/86	
	Decreto-lei N.396/86, 25/11/86	
	Decreto-lei N.154/88, 29/04/88	
	Decreto Regulamentar N.9/88, 03/03/88	

S	Jämställdhetslag	Svensk författningssamling 1991:433

UK	Equal Pay (Northern Ireland) Act. 1970 (C.41)	
	Equal Pay Act, 1971	
	Social Security (Northern Ireland) Act, 1975 (C.15)	
	Sex Discrimination Act, 1975 (C65)	
	Social Security Act, 1975 (C.14)	
	Sex Discrimination Order 1976	Statutory Rules of Northern Ireland N.1042, 1976
	Sex Discrimination Act, 1986 (C59)	
	Sex Discrimination (Amendment) Order 1988	Statutory Instrument N.249, 1988

SOCIAL PROTECTION

Protection of pregnant women and women who have recently given birth and women who are brestfeeding

Council Directive 92/85/EEC of 19 October 1992, concerning the implementation of measures to encourage improvements in the safety and health of pregnant workers, women workers who have recently given birth and women who are breastfeeding. (Tenth individual Directive within the meaning of Article 16(1) of Directive 89/391/EEC.)

1) Deadline for implementation of the legislation in the Member States

19.10.94

2) References

Official Journal L 348, 28.11.92

A	Mutterschutsgesetz 1979 (MSchG)	Bundesgesetzblatt für die Republik Österreich, Nr.221, idF BGB1 Nr.434/95
	Landarbeitsgesetz 1984	Bundesgesetzblatt für die Republik Österreich, Nr.287, idF BGB1 Nr.514/94
	Kundmachung des Reichsstatthalters in Österreich, wodurch die Berordnung zur Einführung von Arbeitszeitvorschriften im Lande Österreich vom 7/2/39 bekanntgemacht wird (Arbeitszeitordnung)	Bundesgesetzblatt Nr.231/39
	Verordnung des Bundesministers für Soziale verwaltung vom 25/7/73 über den Schutz des Lebens und der Gesundheit der Arbeitnehmer bei Arbeiten in Druckluft sowie bei Taucherarbeiten	Bundesgesetzblatt für die Republik Österreich Nr.501/73, idF BGB1 450/94
	Bundesgesetz, mit dem arbeitsvertragsrechtliche Bestimmungen an das EG-Recht angepasst und das Hausgehilfen- und Hausangestelltengesetz geändert werden	Bundesgesetzblatt für die Republik Österreich Nr.459/93, idF BGB1 NR.450/94
	Allgemeines Sozialversicherungsgesetz (ASVG)	Bundesgesetzblatt für die Republik Österreich Nr 189/55, idF BGB1 Nr.895/95
	Liste der Berufskrankheiten, Anlage 1 zum ASVG Bundesgesetz vom 7/3/85 über die Arbeits- und Sozialgerichtsbarkeit	Bundesgesetzblatt für die Republik Österreich Nr 104/85, idF BGB1 Nr.133/95

B	Articles 39-45 de la Loi du 16/3/71, modifiée par la Loi du 3/4/95 et l'Arrêté Royal du 2/5/95	Moniteur belge 30/3/71 Moniteur belge 10/5/95

D	Gesetz sui Änderung des Mutterschuterechtz 20/12/96 Verorchnung zur enginieden Tunsetzung der EG - Mutterschutz, 15/4/97	Bundesgesetzblatt 30/12/96 p 2110 Bundesgesetzblatt 18/4/97 p 782

DK	Lov N.646, 18/12/85 Lov N.852, 20/12/89 Lov N.686, 11/10/90 Bekendtgørelse N.1181, 18/12/92 Lov N.412, N.447, 01/06/94 Bekendtgørelse N.867, 13/10/94	Lovtidende, 18/12/85 Lovtidende, 20/12/89 Lovtidende, 11/10/90 Lovtidende, 18/12/92 Lovtidende, 01/06/94 Lovtidende, 13/10/94

E	Orden, 09/03/71 Real Decreto N.2065/74, 30/03/74 Ley N.8/80, 10/03/80 Ley N.8/88, 07/04/88 Ley N.3/89, 03/03/89 Real Decreto N.521/90, 27/04/90	Boletín Oficial del Estado, 16/03/71 Boletín Oficial del Estado, 22/07/74 Boletín Oficial del Estado, 14/03/80 Boletín Oficial del Estado, 15/04/88 Boletín Oficial del Estado, 08/03/89 Boletín Oficial del Estado, 02/05/90

EL	Loi N.1568, 11/10/85 Loi N.1302/82 Loi N.1483/84 Loi N.1414/84 Loi N.61/75 Décret présidentiel N.94/1987 Loi N.492/76	FEK A N.177, 18/10/85, p.3335

F	Décret N.96/364, 30/04/96	Journal officiel du 2/5/96, p.6613

FIN	Työsopimuslaki 320/70, 30/04/70, muutos 824/94, 16/9/94 Merimieslaki 423/78, 7/6/78	

I	Decreto-legge del 1/10/96 n.511 Legge del 18/1/72 n.1204 Decreto legislativo del 25/11/96 N.645	Gazzetta Ufficiale 2/10/96 n.231 p.23 Gazzetta Ufficiale 21/12/96 n.299 p.17

IRL	The Safety, Health and Welfare at Work (Pregnant Employees etc.) Regulations 1994	Statutory Instruments N.446 of 1994

L		

NL	Koninklijk Besluit, 02/05/94	Staatsblad N.337, 1994

P	Decreto-Lei 333/95 du 23/12/95	Diário Da República, I Série-A, N.295 du 23/12/95

S	Arbetsmiljölag, Arbetsmiljöförordning,	Svensk författningssamling (SFS) 1977:1160, ändring SFS 1994:579 Svenskförfattningssamling (SFS) 1977:1166, ändring SFS 1994:580

UK	Employment Protection Act 1978 (consolidation) Turera 1993 Commencement Order 1994 Maternity Regulations 1994 (Compulsory Leave) Suspension from Work (on Maternity Grounds) Order 1994	

EQUAL TREATMENT FOR WOMEN AND MEN

Parental leave and leave for family reasons

Council Directive 96/34/EC of 3 June 1996 on the framework agreement on parental leave concluded by UNICE, CEEP and the ETUC.

1) Deadline for implementation of the legislation in the Member States

03.06.98

2) References

Official Journal L 145, 19.06.96

A		

B	Convention collective de travail N 64 du Conseil National du Travail instituant un droit au congé parental, 29/4/97	

D		

DK		

E		
EL		
F		
FIN		
I		
IRL		
L		
NL		

P		
S		
UK		

FREE MOVEMENT FOR WORKERS - MOVEMENT AND RESIDENCE OF WORKERS

Coordination of special measures - public policy, public security and public health

Council Directive 64/221/EEC of 25 February 1964 on the coordination of special measures concerning the movement and residence of foreign nationals which are justified on grounds of public policy, public security or public health.

1) Deadline for implementation of the legislation in the Member States

19.09.1964

2) References

Official Journal L 56, 04.04.64

A	Fremdengesetz Passgesetz 1992 Allgemeines Verwaltungsverfahrengesetz Bundesgesetz Strafregistergesetz	Bundesgesetzblatt N.838/1992 Bundesgesetzblatt N.839/1992 Bundesgesetzblatt N.51/1991 Bundesgesetzblatt N.277/1968, idf.BDGl.N.257/1993

B	Loi du/Wet van 15/12/80	Moniteur Belge du/Belgisch Staatsblad van 31/12/80

D	Gesetz, 31/01/80	Bundesgesetzblatt (Teile I, II, II) S.5, 06/02/80

DK	Bekendtgørelse N.196 Lov, 23/05/80	Lovtidende 23/05/80

E	Décret Royal 766/92, modifié par le D.R. 737/95	

EL	Décret présidentiel N.523/83	Journal Officiel, Volume A

F	Décret N.79-1051, 23/11/79 Décret N.81-405, 28/04/81	Journal officiel N.284, p.3082, 07/12/79 Journal officiel N.101, p.1208, 29/04/81

FIN	Ulkomaaloaislaki (378/91),22/02/91 Laki ulkomaalaislain muuttamisesta (640/93), 28/06/93 Asetus ulkomaalaislain muuttamisesta annetun lain voimaanpanosta (393/93), 22/12/93	

I	Decreto presidenziale N.1656, 30/12/65	Supplemento Ordinario alla Gazetta Ufficiale N.55, 03/03/66

IRL	European Community (Aliens) Regulations 1977-1985	

L	Règlement Grand Ducal 10/01/81	Mémorial A N.3, 30/01/81

NL	Koninklijk Besluit, 24/11/77	Staatsblad N.630/77, 06/12/77

P	Decreto-Lei 60/93, 3/3/93 (Ch. IV, art.12 et suivants)	

S	Regeringsformen Lag om polisregister Rättshjälpslag Passlag Förvaltningslag Utlänningslag Utlänningsförordning Förordning om ändring i förordningen (1992:1166) om ändring i utlänningsförordningen (1989:529)	Svensk förmattningssamling(SFS) 1965:94 Svensk förmattningssamling(SFS) 1972:429 Svensk förmattningssamling(SFS) 1978:302 Svensk förmattningssamling(SFS) 1986:223 Svensk förmattningssamling(SFS) 1989:529, ändring SFS 1992:1165 Svensk förmattningssamling(SFS) 1989:547, ändring SFS 1992:1166 Svensk förmattningssamling(SFS) 1993:1369

UK	Statement of Immigration Rules Control Entry 01/1973 Statement of Changes in Immigration Rules, 1980 Statement of Changes in Immigration Rules, 1983	Statutory Instrument, 25/01/73 Statutory Instrument, 20/02/80 Statutory Instrument, 09/02/83

FREE MOVEMENT OF WORKERS - MOVEMENT AND RESIDENCE OF WORKERS

Abolition of restrictions on movement and residence - Directive 68/360/EEC

Council Directive 68/360/EEC of 15 October 1968 on the abolition of restrictions on movement and residence within the Community for workers of Member States and their families.

1) Deadline for implementation of the legislation in the Member States

16.07.1969

2) References

Official Journal L 257, 19.10.68

A	Erlassung des Fremdengesetzes und Änderung des Asylgesetzes 1991, sowie des Aufenthaltsgesetzes	Bundesgesetzblatt N.838/1992
	Meldegesetz 1991	Bundesgesetzblatt N.9/1992, idF. DGBl. N.520/1993
	Passgesetz 1992, 29.12.1992	Bundesgesetzblatt N.839/1992
	Ausländerbeschäftigungsgesetz	Bundesgesetzblatt N.218/1975, idF. DGBl.N.709/1993
	Gebührengesetz 1957	Bundesgesetzblatt N.267/1957, idF. DGBl.N.780/1992
	Bundesverwaltungsabgabenverordnung 21/12/83	Bundesgesetzblatt N.24/1983, idF. DGBl.N.151/1992

B	Arrêté Royal du/Koninklijk Besluit van 13/05/68	Moniteur Belge du/Belgisch Staatsblad van 14/08/68, p.6675
	Arrêté Royal du/Koninklijk Besluit van 11/07/69	Moniteur Belge du/Belgisch Staatsblad van 14/08/69, p.7760
	Circulaire du Ministère de la Justice/Omzendbrief van de Ministerie van Justitie, 14/08/69	Moniteur Belge du/Belgisch Staatsblad van 14/08/69, p.7773
	Circulaire du Ministère de laJustice/Omzendbrief van de Ministerie van Justitie, 01/03/77	Moniteur Belge du/Belgisch Staatsblad van 18/03/77, p.3371
	Loi du/Wet van 15/12/80	Moniteur Belge du/Belgisch Staatsblad

	Arrêté Royal du/Koninklijk Besluit van 08/10/81 Loi du 28/06/84 modifiant L du 15/12/80/Wet van 28/06/84 tot wijziging van 15/12/80 Arrêté Royal du 16/08/84 modifiant A.R. du 08/10/81/Koninklijk Besluit van 16/08/84 tot wijziging van K.B. van 08/10/81	van 31/12/80 Moniteur Belge du/Belgisch Staatsblad van 27/10/81 Moniteur Belge du/Belgisch Staatsblad van 12/07/84 Moniteur Belge du/Belgisch Staatsblad van 01/09/84
D	Gesetz über Einreise und Aufenthalt von Staatsangehörigen der EWG, 22/07/69 Änderung des Gesetz über Einreise und Aufenthalt von Staatsangehoerigen der EWG, 1974 Gesetz, 31/01/80 Gesetz, 11/09/81 Gesetz, 09/07/90	Bundesgesetzblatt Teil I S.927, 22/07/69 Bundesgesetzblatt Teil I S.948, 17/04/74 Bundesgesetzblatt Teil I, N.5, S.113, 06/02/80 Bundesgesetzblatt Teil I S.949, 1981 Bundesgesetzblatt Teil I S.1379, 1990
DK	Lov N.155, 21/03/73 Bekendtgørelse N.346, 22/06/73 Vedtægt N.226, 08/06/83 Bekendtgørelse N.19, 18/01/84 Bekendtgørelse N.20, 18/01/84	Lovtidende A, 21/03/73 Lovtidende A, 22/06/73
E	Real Decreto N.1099/86, 26/05/86	Boletín Oficial del Estado N.139, 11/06/86
EL	Décret présidentiel N.525, 1983 Circulaire N.112979, 24/12/87 Décret présidentiel N.499, 31/12/87 Circulaire N.110886, 04/11/88 Décret présidentiel N.308, 30/06/91	Journal Officiel N.203, Volume A, 31/12/83 Journal Officiel N.238, Volume A, 31/12/87 Journal Officiel N.106, Volume A, 10/07/91

F	Décret N.70-29, 05/01/70	Journal Officiel p.516, 05/01/70
	Circulaire - conditions de séjour en France ressortissants CEE, 24/01/72	Journal Officiel p.1790, 18/02/72
	Arrêté ministériel, 09/11/72	Journal Officiel
	Décret N.79-1051, 23/11/79	Journal Officiel N.284, p.3082, 07/12/79
	Décret N.81-405, 28/04/81	Journal Officiel p.1208, 29/04/81
	Décret N.94-211, 11/03/94	Journal Officiel p.3989 - 3992, 13/03/94

FIN	Ulkomaaloaislaki (378/91),22/02/91	
	Laki ulkomaalaislain muuttamisesta (640/93), 28/06/93	
	Asetus ulkomaalaislain muuttamisesta annetun lain voimaanpanosta (393/93), 22/12/93	

I	Decreto presidenziale N.1656, 30/12/65	Gazzetta Ufficiale N.55, 03/03/66
	Decreto presidenziale N.1225 - modifica del DP N.65-1656, 29/12/69	Gazzetta Ufficiale N.75, 25/03/70

IRL	European Community (Aliens) Regulations 1972	Statutory Instrument N.333, 1972
	European Community (Aliens)(Amendment) Order 1975	Statutory Instrument N.128, 1975
	European Community (Aliens) Regulations 1977	Statutory Instrument N.393, 1977
	European Community (Aliens)(Amendment) Order 1978	Statutory Instrument N.351, 1978

L	Règlement Grand Ducal, 28/03/72	Mémorial A, p.826, 1972
	Loi, 16/04/75	Mémorial A N.26, 07/05/75
	Règlement Grand Ducal, 29/08/76	Mémorial A N.56, p.956, 16/09/76
	Règlement Grand Ducal, 10/01/81	Mémorial A N.3, p.36, 30/01/81

NL	Koninklijk Besluit art.91-102a, 19/09/66	Staatsblad N.387, 1966
	Beschikking van de Minister vanJustitie, art.4, 31, 34 en 48, 22/09/66	
	Koninklijk Besluit N.1, 15/07/69	Staatsblad N.305, 1969
	Koninklijk Besluit, 28/05/74	Staatsblad N.349, 1974
	Ministeriële Beschikking, 28/05/74	Staascourant N.127, 1974
	Vreemdelingenomzendbrief 1984	

P	Decreto-lei N.264/B/81, 03/09/81	Diário da República I Serie N.202, 03/09/81
	Decreto-lei N.333/82, 19/08/82	Diário da República I Serie N.191, 19/08/82
	Decreto-lei N.312/86, 24/09/86	Diário da República I Serie N.220, 24/09/86
	Decreto-lei N.267/87, 02/07/87	Diário da República I Serie N.149, 02/07/87
	Portaria N.482/88, 23/07/88	Diário da República I Serie N.169, 23/07/88

S	Regeringsformen	
	Passlag	Svensk förmattningssamling(SFS) 1978:302
	Förvaltningslag	Svensk förmattningssamling(SFS) 1986:223
	Utlänningslag	Svensk förmattningssamling(SFS)1989:529, ändring SFS 1992:1165
	Utlänningsförordning	Svensk förmattningssamling(SFS) 1989:547, ändring SFS 1992:1166
	Förordning om ändring i förordningen (1992:1166) om ändring I utlänningsförordningen (1989:529)	Svensk förmattningssamling(SFS) 1993:1369

UK	Immigration Act 1971	
	Statement of Immigration Rules	Statutory Instrument 1973
	Control Entry, 1973	
	Statement of Changes Immigration Rules 1980	Statutory Instrument N.394, 1980
	Statement of Changes Immigration Rules 1983	Statutory Instrument N.169, 1983

FREE MOVEMENT FOR WORKERS

Right to remain in the territory of a Member State

Council Directive 72/194/EEC of 18 May 1972 extending to workers exercising the right to remain in the territory of a Member State and having been employed in that State, the scope of the Directive of 25 February 1964 on coordination of special measures concerning the movement and residence of foreign nationals which are justified on grounds of public policy, public security or public health.

1) Deadline for implementation of the legislation in the Member States

23.11.1972

2) References

Official Journal L 121, 26.05.72

A	Fremdengesetz	Bundesgesetzblatt N.838/1992

B	Loi du/Wet van 28/03/52	Moniteur Belge du/Belgisch Staatsblad van 30/03/52
	Loi du 30/04/64 modifiant L du28/03/52 Wet van 30/04/64 tot wijziging van het Wet van 28/03/52	Moniteur Belge du/Belgisch Staatsblad van 30/06/64, p.7270
	Arrêté Royal du 13/05/68 modifiant l'A.R. du 21/12/65/Koninklijk Besluit van 13/05/68 tot wijziging van het K.B. van 21/12/65	Moniteur Belge du/Belgisch Staatsblad van 14/06/68, p.6675
	Loi du 01/04/69 modifiant Loi du 28/03/52 Wet van 01/04/69 tot wijziging van het Wet van 28/03/52	Moniteur Belge du/Belgisch Staatsblad van 20/06/69, p.6182
	Arrêté Royal du 11/07/69 modifiant l'A.R. du 21/12/65/Koninklijk Besluit van 11/07/69 tot wijziging van het K.B. van 21/12/65	Moniteur Belge du/Belgisch Staatsblad van 14/08/69, p.7760
	Loi du 31/05/71 modifiant Loi du 28/03/52/Wet van 31/05/71 tot wijziging van het Wet van 28/03/52	Moniteur Belge du/Belgisch Staatsblad van 08/10/76, p.12921
	Circulaire du/Omzendbrief van 05/10/76	Moniteur Belge du/Belgisch Staatsblad van 08/10/76, p.12921
	Circulaire du Ministère de la Justice/Omzendbrief van de Ministerie van Justitie, 01/03/77	Moniteur Belge du/Belgisch Staatsblad van 18/03/77, p.3371

D	Rundschreiben	Bundesgesetzblatt Teil I, 22/01/73

DK	Lov N.155, 21/03/73	Lovtidende, 21/03/73
	Bekendtgørelse N.346, 22/06/73	Lovtidende, 22/06/73

E	Ley N.155, 21/03/73	Boletín Oficial del Estado 02/07/85
	Real Decreto N.1099/86, 11/06/86	Boletín Oficial del Estado, 11/06/86
	Real Decreto N.1119/86, 12/06/86	Boletín Oficial del Estado, 12/06/86
	Real Decreto N.116/88, 05/02/88	Boletín Oficial del Estado, 19/02/88
	Corrección de errores del R.D. N.1119/86	Boletín Oficial del Estado, 23/07/86

EL	Décret présidentiel N.499, 31/12/87	Journal Officiel N.238, Volume A, p.4010, 16/06/89

F	Décret N.77-957, 19/08/77	Journal Officiel, 24/08/77

FIN	Ulkomaaloaislaki (378/91),22/02/91 Laki ulkomaalaislain muuttamisesta (640/93), 28/06/93 Asetus ulkomaalaislain muuttamisesta annetun lain voimaanpanosta (393/93), 22/12/93	

I	Legge N.128, 04/04/77	Gazzetta Ufficiale N.115, 19/04/77

IRL	European Community (Aliens) Regulations 1972 European Community (Aliens) Regulations 1977	Statutory Instrument N.333, 1972 Statutory Instrument N.393, 1977

L	Règlement Grand Ducal, 28/03/72 Réglement Grand Ducal, 28/08/76	Mémorial A, N.24, 13/04/72 Mémorial A, N.56, 17/09/76

NL	Koninklijk Besluit, 27/11/72 Koninklijk Besluit, 24/02/76 tot Wijziging van het K.B. van 27/11/72	Staatsblad N.615, 27/11/72 Staatsblad N.630, 24/02/76

P	Decreto-lei N.264/B/81, 03/09/81 Decreto-lei N.267/87, 02/07/87	Diário da República I Serie N.202, 03/09/81 Diário da República I Serie N.149, 02/07/87

S	Regeringsformen	
	Lag om polisregister	Svensk förmattningssamling(SFS) 1965:94
	Rättshjälpslag	Svensk förmattningssamling(SFS) 1972:429
	Passlag	Svensk förmattningssamling(SFS) 1978:302
	Förvaltningslag	Svensk förmattningssamling(SFS) 1986:223
	Utlänningslag	Svensk förmattningssamling(SFS) 1989:529, ändring SFS 1992:1165
	Utlänningsförordning	Svensk förmattningssamling(SFS) 1989:547, ändring SFS 1992:1166
	Förordning om ändring i förordningen (1992:1166) om ändring I utlänningsförordningen (1989:529)	Svensk förmattningssamling(SFS) 1993:1369

UK	Statement of Changes Immigration Rules 1980	Statutory Instrument N.394, 1980
	Statement of Changes Immigration Rules 1983	Statutory Instrument N.169, 1983

HEALTH AND SAFETY AT WORK - DANGEROUS AGENTS

Exposure to vinyl chloride monomer

Council Directive 78/610/EEC of 29 June 1978 on the approximation of the laws, regulations and administrative provisions of the Member States on the protection of the health of workers exposed to vinyl chloride monomer.

1) Deadline for implementation of the legislation in the Member States

05.01.1980

2) References

Official Journal L 197, 22.07.1978

A	Bundesgesetz über Sicherheit und Gesundheit bei der Arbeit	Bundesgesetzblatt N.450/1994, 17/06/94

B	Arrêté Royal /Koninklijk Besluit	Moniteur Belge du/Belgisch Staatsblad van 02/08/80

D	Verordnung über gefährliche Arbeitsstoffe, 29/07/80	Bundesgesetzblatt (Teile I), 07/09/80

DK	No VCH production	

E	Orden, 09/04/86	Boletín Oficial del Estado N.108, 06/05/86

EL	Décret Présidentiel, N.1179	Journal Officiel N.302, Volume A, 30/12/80

F	Décret N.80-203, 12/03/80	Journal Officiel, 12/03/80

FIN	Valtioneuvosten päätös vinyylikloridyöstä (919/92), 08/10/92	Suomen Säädöskokoelma

I	Decreto del Presidente della Republica N.962, 10/09/82	Gazzetta Ufficiale N.5, 06/01/83

IRL	Not applicable	

L	Loi, 22/07/82	Doc parl N 2590; sess ord 1981-1982

NL	Besluit van 03/06/82	Staatsblad N.433, 1982

P	Decreto-lei N.273/89, 21/08/89	Diário da República, 21/08/89

S	Arbetsmiljölag Arbetsmiljöförordning	Svensk författningssamling 1977:1160 Svensk författningssamling 1977:1166 Arbetarskyddsstyrelsens författningssamling (AFS) 1980:11, AFS 1985:17,AFS 1988:3, AFS 1990:13, AFS 1993:9,37

UK	Control of Substances Hazardous to Health Regulations 1988	Statutory Instruments 1998/1657

HEALTH AND SAFETY AT WORK - DANGEROUS AGENTS

Exposure to chemical, physical and biological agents.

Council Directive 80/1107/EEC of 27 November 1980 on the protection of workers from the risks related to exposure to chemical, physical and biological agents at work.

Council Directive 88/642/EEC of 16 December 1988 amending Directive 80/1107/EEC on the protection of workers from the risks related to exposure to chemical, physical and biological agents at work.

Commission Directive 91/322/EEC of 29 May 1991 on establishing indicative limit values by implementing Council Directive 80/1107/EEC on the protection of workers from the risks related to exposure to chemical, physical and biological agents at work

Commission Directive 96/94/EC of 18 December 1996 on establishing indicative limit values by implementing Council Directive 80/1107/EEC on the protection of workers from the risks related to exposure to chemical, physical and biological agents at work

1) Deadline for implementation of the legislation in the member states

Directive 80/1107/EEC: 05.12.1983

Directive 88/642/EEC: 21.12.1990

Directive 91/322/EEC: 31.12.1993

Directive 96/94/EC: 01.06.1998

2) References

Official Journal L 327, 03.12.1980

Official Journal L 356, 24.12.1988

Official Journal L 177, 05.07.1991

Official Journal L 338, 28.12.1996

A	ArbeitnehmerInnenschutzgesetz - ASchG	Bundesgesetzblatt N.450/1994, 17/06/94

| B | Arrêté Royal du/Koninklijk Besluit van 10/04/74
Arrêté Royal du/Koninklijk Besluit van 20/11/87
Arrêté royal modifiant le règlement général pour la protection du travailleur en ce qui concerne la fixation des valeurs limites d'exposition à des agents chimiques 11/4/95
Arrêté Royal du/Koninklijk Besluit van 18/12/91 insérant dans le règlement général pour la protection du travail la directive 88/642/CEE | Moniteur Belge du/Belgisch Staatsblad van 08/05/75, p.6718
Moniteur Belge du/Belgisch Staatsblad van 27/11/87, p.176
Moniteur belge n°95 14/6/95 p 1608

Moniteur Belge du/Belgisch Staatsblad van 01/02/92 p 2143 |

| D | Verordnung über gefährliche Stoffe 25/09/86
Zweiten verordnung zur Anderung der Gafahrstoffuerurdnung 23/4/90
Verordnung über gefährliche Stoffe - Gefahrstoffverordnung in der Fassung 25/09/91 | Bundesgesetzblatt Teil I, S.1931
Bundesgesetzblatt I S 790

Bundesgesetzblatt Teil I, S.1931 |

| DK | Lov N.681, 23/12/75
Vejledning nr 87/1979
Anvisning nr 62/1976
Arbejdsministeriet bekendtgørelse nr 321 af 2/6/77
Bekendtgørelse N.540, 02/09/82
Bekendtgørelse N.323, 07/07/83
Lov N.646, 18/12/85 |

Lovtidende A, 02/09/82
Lovtidende A, 07/07/83
Lovtidende A, 18/12/85 |

| E | Orden 09/05/62
Orden 09/03/71
Ley N.8/80, 10/03/80
Ley N.11/85, 02/08/85 | Boletín Oficial del Estado
Boletín Oficial del Estado, 16/03/71
Boletín Oficial del Estado, 14/03/80
Boletín Oficial del Estado |

EL	Décret présidentiel N.307 Décret présidentiel N.77, 03/03/93	Journal Officiel N.177, Volume A, 18/10/85 FEK A N.34, 18/03/93 p.339

F	Code du Travail, Titre 4, Livre 2 Arrêté Ministériel du 11/07/77 Décret N.84-1093 Circulaire	Journal Officiel 24/07/77 Journal Officiel 08/12/84 Journal Officiel p.6269, 06/06/85

FIN	Valtioneuvosten päätös työntekijöiden suojelemisesta kemiallisille tekijöille altistumiseen liittyviltä vaaroilta (920/92), 08/10/92, muutos (727/93), 29/07/93	Suomen Säädöskokoelma Bilaga p.2399

I	Decreto presidenziale N.547, 27/04/55	Supplemento Ordinario alla Gazzetta Ufficiale N.158, 12/07/55
	Decreto presidenziale N.303, 19/03/56	Supplemento Ordinario alla Gazzetta Ufficiale N.105, 30/04/56
	Decreto presidenziale N.1124, 30/06/65	Supplemento Ordinario alla Gazzetta Ufficiale N.257, 13/10/65
	Legge N.604, 15/07/66	Gazzetta Ufficiale N.195, 06.08.66
	Legge N.300, 20/05/70	Gazzetta Ufficiale N.131, 27.05.70
	Legislative Decreto N.277, 15/08/91	Gazzetta Ufficiale N.53, 27/08/91

IRL	Factories (Carcinogenic Substance) (Processes) Regulations 1972 Safety, Health and Welfare at Work (Chemical Agents) Regulations 1994 National Authority for Occupational Safety and Health, Code of Practice (C.P. N.1 of 1994) for the Safety, Health and Welfare at Work (Chemical Agents) Regulations 1994	Statutory Instrument N.242 of 1972 Statutory Instruments N.445, 1994 Statutory Instruments N.445, 1994

L	Loi, 20/05/88 Loi du 19/07/91 concernant la protection des travailleurs contre les risques liés à l'exposition à des agents chimiques, biologiques et physiques pendant le travail	Mémorial A N.24, 27/05/88 Receuil de législation, A-N.49, 02/08/91, p.996
NL	Wet Arbeidsomstandigheden, 1980 Besluit 18/03/85	Staatsblad N.664, 1980 Staatsblad N.212, 1985
P	Decreto-lei N.479/85	Diário da República
S	Arbetsmiljölag Arbetsmiljöförordning	Svensk författningssamling 1977:1160 Svensk författningssamling 1977:1166 Arbetarskyddsstyrelsens författningssamling (AFS) 1980:11, ändring AFS93:7 Arbetarskyddsstyrelsens författningssamling (AFS) 1980:12, AFS 1981:9, AFS 1983:11, AFS 1984:8,15, AFS 1985:1 1985:17, AFS 1986:7,13,28, AFS 1987:2, AFS 1988:5, ändring AFS 1991:9, AFS 1988:3,6, AFS1989:2,3, AFS 1990:9, 1990:13,14, AFS 1992:2,10,16,17, AFS 1993:4,5,9,37

UK	Health and Safety at Work Act 1974 Chapter 37, Reprinted 1980	
	The Representatives and Safety Commit. Regululations 1977	Statutory Instrument N.500, 1977
	Guidance note EH 8 The Health and Safety Executive Arsenic	Statutory Instrument 1977
	Guidance note EH 11 the Health and Safety Executive Arsine	Statutory Instrument 1977
	Guidance note EH 1 the Health and Safety Executive Cadmium	Statutory Instrument 1977
	Guidance note EH 17 The Health and Safety Executive Mercury	Statutory Instrument 1977
	Leaflet MS(A) 1 The Health and Safety Executive Lead and Youth Employment Protection (Consolidation) Act 1978 Chapt.44	
	The Safety Repres. of Safety Committees Regulations 1979 (Northern Ireland)	Statutory Instrument N.437, 1979
	Guidance Notes Health & Safety Agency (Northern Ireland) Leaflet HSA6	
	Guidance Notes Health & Safety Agency (N.I.) Leaflet HSA 15	
	The Health & Safety at Work (Northern Ireland) Order 1978	Statutory Rules of Northern Ireland N.1039, 1978
	The Industrial Relations (NO 2) (Northern Ireland) Order 1978	Statutory Rules of Northern Ireland N.2147, 1978
	The Control of Lead and Work Regulations 1980	Statutory Rules of Northern Ireland N.1248, 1980 2nd Edition 1983
	Guidance Note EH 10 Health and Safety Executive Asbestos	
	Codpr. Work with Asbestos Insulation and Asbestos Coating	Statutory Instrument, 13/06/83
	The Asbestos (licencing) Regulations 1983 The Asbestos (licencing)	Statutory Rules of Northern Ireland N.1649, 1983
	Regulations 1984 Northern Ireland	Statutory Instrument 1984
	Health and Safety, The Control of Substances Hazardous to Health Regulations 1988 26/9/1988	Statutory Instrument 1988, p.1657

PROTECTION OF SAFETY AND HEALTH AT WORK – WORKPLACES AND CATEGORIES OF WORKERS PARTICULARLY AT RISK

Electrical equipment for use in potentially explosive atmospheres in mines susceptible to firedamp

Council Directive 82/130/EEC of 15 February 1982 on the approximation of the laws of the Member States concerning electrical equipment for use in potentially explosive atmospheres in mines susceptible to firedamp.

Commission Directive 88/35/EEC of 2 December 1987 adapting to technical progress Council Directive 82/130/EEC on the approximation of the laws of the Member States concerning electrical equipment for use in potentially explosive atmospheres in mines susceptible to firedamp.

Commission Directive 91/269/EEC of 30 April 1991 adapting to technical progress Council Directive 82/130/EEC on the approximation of the laws of the Member States concerning electrical equipment for use in potentially explosive atmospheres in mines susceptible to firedamp.

Commission Directive 94/44/EEC of 19 September 1994 adapting to technical progress Council Directive 82/130/EEC on the approximation of the laws of the Member States concerning electrical equipment for use in potentially explosive atmospheres in mines susceptible to firedamp.

1) Deadline for implementation of the legislation in the Member States

Directive 82/130/EEC: 19.08.1983

Directive 88/35/EEC: 01.01.1988

Directive 91/269/EEC: 29.06.1992

Directive 94/44/EEC: 30.09.1995

2) References

Official Journal L 59, 02.03.1982

Official Journal L 20, 26.01.1988

Official Journal L 134, 29.05.1991

Official Journal L 248, 23.09.1994

A	Verordnung über elektrische Betriebsmittel zur Verwendung in Schlagwettergefährdeten Grubenbauen	Bundesgesetzblatt N.53/95 17/1/95

B	Arrêté Royal 21/12/83 Arrêté Royal 29/7/94 Arrêté Royal 1/9/95	Moniteur belge 7/2/84 Moniteur belge 3/9/94 p.22491 Moniteur belge 28/9/95 p.27531

D	Bergverordnung vom 21/12/83 Bekanntmachung vom 10/10/91 Zweite verordnung zur Änderung der Elektrozulassungs-Bergverordnung vom 10/12/92 Bekanntmachung vom 1/12/94	Bundesgesetzblatt Teil I N.54 28/12/83 Bundesanzeiger 5/11/91 S.7345 Bundesgesetzblatt Teil I Seite 2010 Bundesanzeiger N.233 vom 13/12/94

DK	Bekendtgørelse N.660 af 28/12/77 Strakstrømreglementer	

E	Reglamento N.863/85 Orden N.2635 de 20/1/94 Orden de 3/4/92 Corrección de erratas de la orden de 3/4/92 Orden de 11/10/96 por la que se modifican las instrucciones técnicas complementarias 12.0.01 y 12.0.02 del Reglamento General de Normas Básicas de Seguridad Minera Corrección de erratas de la orden de 11/10/96 23/10/96	Boletín oficial del Estado N.140, 12/6/85 Boletín oficial del Estado N.30, 4/2/94 p.3667 Boletín oficial del Estado N.99, 24/4/92 Boletín oficial del Estado N.133, 3/6/92 Boletín oficial del Estado N.256, 23/10/96 p.31684 Boletín oficial del Estado N.312 27/12/96 p.38541

EL	Décision ministérielle N.13353/2636 28/2/90 Décision ministérielle N.19849/4370 29/9/92	FEK B N.442 20/7/90 p.5865 FEK B N.599/1992

F	Arrêté ministériel du 23/11/82 Arrêté ministériel du 11/10/91 Arrêté ministériel du 17/1/95	Journal officiel 29/1/83 Journal officiel 28/11/91 p.15498 Journal officiel 4/3/95 p.3458

FIN	Not applicable	

I	Decreto ministeriale del 1/3/83 Decreto ministeriale del 8/4/91 N.228 Decreto del 10/8/94 N.587 Decreto del 1/7/97	Gazzetta Ufficiale del 17/3/83 N.75 p.2085 Gazzetta Ufficiale del 31/7/91 N.178 Gazzetta Ufficiale del 22/10/94 N.248 Gazzetta Ufficiale N.158 del 9/7/97, p.10

IRL	(Water pollution) (Amendment) Order of 25/9/92 (Water Pollution) Order of 25/9/92 (Water Pollution) Regulations of 1992	Statutory Instruments N.270 of 1992 Statutory Instruments N.272 of 1992 Statutory Instruments N.271 of 1992

L	Règlement Grand-Ducal 13/8/92 Règlement Grand-Ducal du 30/4/93 Règlement Grand-Ducal du 20/4/95	Mémorial Grand-Ducal A P.2160 Mémorial Grand-Ducal A N.39 du 1/6/93 p.776 Mémorial Grand-Ducal A N.42 du 23/5/95 p.1183

NL	Regeling in zake afgifte certificaten met betrekking tot electrisch materieel bestemd voor gebruik in explosieve omgeving van mijngashoudende mijnen 17/12/91 Regeling afgifte certificaten met betrekking tot electrisch materieel bestemd voor gebruik in explosieve omgeving van mijngashoudende mijnen	Staatscourant N.249 van 23/12/91 Staatscourant N.18 van 25/1/95

P	Not applicable	

S	Not applicable	

UK	Mines (Miscellaneus Amendments) Regulations of 1983	Statutory instruments N.1130 of 1983
	The Electrical Equipment for Explosive Atmospheres (Certification) Regulations of 1990	Statutory Instruments N.13 of 1990
	The Electrical Equipment for Explosive Atmospheres (Certification) Regulations of 1990 (Northern Ireland)	Statutory Rules of Northern Ireland N.284 of 1990
	The Electricity at Work Regulations of 1989	Statutory Instruments N.635 of 1989
	The Electricity at Work Regulations (Northern Ireland) of 1991	Statutory Rules of Northern Ireland N.13 of 1991
	The Electrical Equipment for Explosive Atmospheres (Certification)(Amendment) N.2 Regulations of 12/12/91	Statutory Instruments N.2826 of 1991
	The Electrical Equipment for Explosive Atmospheres (Certification)(Amendment) Regulations (Northern Ireland)of 20/7/92	Statutory Rules of Northern Ireland N.256 of 1992
	The Electrical Equipment for Explosive Atmospheres (Certification)(Amendment) Regulations of 95	Statutory Instruments N.1186 of 1995
	The Electrical Equipment for Explosive Atmospheres (Certification)(Amendment) Regulations (Northern Ireland)of 1995	Statutory Rules of Northern Ireland N.275 of 1995

HEALTH AND SAFETY AT WORK - DANGEROUS AGENTS

Exposure to metallic lead and its ionic compounds

Council Directive 82/605/EEC of 28 July 1982 on the protection of workers from the risks related to exposure to metallic lead and its ionic compounds at work (first individual Directive within the meaning of Article 8 of Directive 80/1107/EEC).

1) Deadline for implementation of the legislation in the Member States

01.01.86

2) References

Official Journal L 247, 23.08.82

A	ArbeitnehmerInnenschutzgesetz - ASchG	Bundesgesetzblatt N.450/1994, 17/06/94

B	Arrêté Royal du/Koninklijk Besluit van 07/11/88	Moniteur Belge du/Belgisch Staatsblad van 22/11/88, p.16119

D	Verordnung Gefahrstoffverordnung vom 26/08/86	Bundesgesetzblatt (Teile I, II, III) I S.1470, 5/9/86

DK	Bekendtgørelse N.392, 10/08/78 Bekendtgørelse N.32, 29/01/79 Bekendtgørelse N.323, 07/07/83 Arbejdsministeriet Bekendtgørelse N.562, 16/12/85	

E	Orden, 09/05/86	Boletín Oficial del Estado N.98, 24/04/86

EL	Décret présidentiel N.94/87, 10/04/87	Journal Officiel N.54, Volume A, p.503, 22/04/87

F	Décret N.88-120, 01/02/88 Arrêté Ministériel, 11/04/88	Journal Officiel, 05/02/88 Journal Officiel, 19/04/88

FIN	Valtioneuvosten päätös lyijytyöstä (1154/93), 09/12/93	

I	Decreto del Presidente della Republica N.303, 19/03/56 Decreto Legge N.227, 15/08/91	Supplemento Ordinario alla Gazzetta Ufficiale N.105, 30/06/56 Gazzetta Ufficiale N.200/91, 27/08/91, p.3

IRL	E.C. (Protection of Workers) (Exposure to Lead) Regulations 1988	Statutory Instrument N.219 of 1988

L	Règlement Grand Ducal, 15/07/88	Mémorial A

NL	Koninklijk Besluit van 18/02/88 (Loodbesluit) Ministeriële Beschikking	Staatsblad N.100, 1988 Staatcourant N.61, 1988

P	Decreto-lei N.274/89, 21/08/89	Diário da República 21/08/89

S	Arbetsmiljölag Arbetsmiljöförordning Arbetarskyddstyrelsens kungörelse med föreskrifter om hygieniska gränsvärden Arbetarskyddstyrelsens kungörelse med föreskrifter om hygieniska gränsvärden	Svensk författningssamling 1977:1160 Svensk författningssamling 1977:1166 Arbetarskyddsstyrelsens författningssamling (AFS) 1992:17 Arbetarskyddsstyrelsens författningssamling (AFS) 1990:13 Arbetarskyddsstyrelsens författningssamling (AFS) 1993:9

UK	Control of Lead (Air Sampling Techniques & Strategies) Health & Safety (Control of Lead) Work Regulation 1986 Control of Lead at Work: Approved Code of Practice.	Guidance Note EH 28 Health & Safety Executive Statutory Rules of Northern Ireland N.36, 1986 Health & Safety Booklet HSA 29 (March 1986)

HEALTH AND SAFETY AT WORK - DANGEROUS AGENTS

Exposure to asbestos

Council Directive 83/477/EEC of 19 September 1983 on the protection of workers from the risks related to exposure to asbestos at work (second individual Directive within the meaning of Article 8 of Directive 80/1107/EEC).

Council Directive 91/382/EEC of 25 June 1991 amending Directive 83/477/EEC on the protection of workers from the risks related to exposure to asbestos at work (second individual Directive within the meaning of Article 8 of Directive 80/1107/EEC).

1) Deadline for implementation of the legislation in the Member States

Directive 83/477/EEC: 01.01.1987

Directive 91/382/EEC: 01.01.1996

2) References

Official Journal L 263, 24.09.1983

Official Journal L 206, 29.07.1991

A	ArbeitnehmerInnenschutzgesetz - ASchG	Bundesgesetzblatt N.450/1994, 17/06/94

B	Arrêté Royal du/Koninklijk Besluit van 28/08/86 Arrêté Royal du/Koninklijk Besluit van 22/07/91	Moniteur Belge du/Belgisch Staatsblad van 19/09/86, N.1412, p.12676 Moniteur Belge du/Belgisch Staatsblad van 25/07/91, p.16438

D	Verordnung Gefahrstoffverordnung vom 26/8/86 Verordnung Gefahrstoffverordnung vom 26/10/93	Bundesgesetzblatt (Teile I, II, III) S.1470, 5/9/86 Bundesgesetzblatt (Teile I, II, III) S.1782; N.57, 30/10/93

DK	Lov N.292, 10/06/81	
	Bekendtgørelse N.660, 24/09/86	Lovtidende, 24/09/86
	Meddelelse, 04/02/87	
	Bekendtgørelse, 11/12/92 om ændr. af bek. om asbest	Lovtidende, 11/12/92
	AT-anvisning N.31, 02/01/92	
	Bekendtgørelse N.855, 06/10/94	Lovtidende, 06/10/94

E	Orden, 31/10/84	
	Resolutíon, 11/02/85	
	Orden, 31/03/86	
	Orden, 07/01/87	Boletín Oficial del Estado N.13, 15/01/87
	Resolutíon, 08/09/87	Boletín Oficial del Estado, 14/10/87
	Orden, 22/12/87	Boletín Oficial del Estado, 29/12/87
	Ley N.8/88, 07/04/88	
	Resolutíon, 20/02/89	
	Real Decreto N.108/91, 01/02/91	Boletín Oficial del Estado N.32, 06/02/91
	Orden, 26/07/93	Boletín Oficial del Estado N.186, 11/08/93

EL	Décret présidentiel N.70A	Journal Officiel B.31 du 17/02/88
	Décret présidentiel du 15/9/97	Journal officiel du 15/8/97 p.6280

F	Décret N.77-949, 17/08/77	Journal Officiel N.217, 18/09/77
	Décret N.87/232, 27/03/87	
	Circulaire DRT N.88/15, 08/08/88	
	Décret N.92-634, 06/07/92	Journal officiel 10/7/92 p 9294

FIN	Valtioneuvosten päätös asbestityösta (886/87) 26/11/87	Suomen Säädöskokoelma

I	Decreto presidenziale N.303, 19/03/56	Supplemento Ordinario alla Gazzetta Ufficiale N.105, 30/04/56
	Decreto presidenziale N.1124, 30/06/65	Supplemento Ordinario alla Gazzetta Ufficiale N.257, 13/10/65
	Legge N.833, 23/12/78	Supplemento Ordinario alla Gazzetta Ufficiale N.360, 28/12/78
	Decreto Legislativo N.277, 15/8/91	Gazzetta Ufficiale, p.3, 27/08/91

| IRL | E.C. (Protection of Workers) (Exposure to Asbestos) Regul. 1989 | Statutory Instrument N.34 of 1989 |
| | E.C. (Protection of Workers) (Exposure to Asbestos) Regul. 1993 | Statutory Instrument N.276 of 1983 |

| L | Règlement Grand-Ducal, 15/07/88 | Memorial A N.46, p.801, 30/07/88 |
| | Règlement Grand Ducal, 21/04/93, modifiant le Règl. du 15/07/88 | Mémorial A N 36, 14/5/93 |

NL	Besluit van Asbest Arbeidsomstandighenwet 10/12/91	Staatsblad 1991, N.685, N.560
	Besluit van 19/02/93 tot wijziging van het Asbestbesluit Arbeidsomstandighedenwet	Staatsblad 1993, N.135
	Beschikking van de Minister van Justitie van 05/03/93, houdende plaatsing in het Staatsblad van de tekst van het Asbestbesluit Arbeidsomstandighedenwet (Stb. 1988, 560), zoals dit alltstelijk is gewijzigd bij koninklijk besluit van 19/02/1993, Stb 135	Staatsblad 1993, N.136
	Besluit van 22/11/88 tot vaststelling van niewe regels ter bescherming van werknemers tegen de risico's van blootstelling aan asbest	Staatsblad 1988, N.560

| P | Decreto-lei N.479/85, 13/11/85 | Diário da República, 13/11/85 |
| | Decreto-lei N.284/89, 24/08/89 | Diario da Republica N.194, p.3540, 24/08/89 |

S	Arbetsmiljölag Arbetsmiljöförordning	Svensk författningssamling 1977:1160 Svensk författningssamling 1977:1166 Arbetarskyddsstyrelsens författnings samling (AFS) 1992:2 Arbetarskyddsstyrelsens författningssamling (AFS) 1990:13 Arbetarskyddsstyrelsens författningssamling (AFS) 1993:9

UK	The Control of Asbestos at Work Regulations, 1987 Health and Safety - The Control of Asbestos at Work (Amendment) Regulations 1992 The Control of Asbestos at Work Regulations, 3/12/1987	Statutory Instrument N.3068, 1987 Statutory Instrument 1992 Statutory Instruments 1987, N.2115

HEALTH AND SAFETY AT WORK - DANGEROUS AGENTS

Exposure to noise

Council Directive 86/188/EEC of 12 May 1986 on the protection of workers from the risks related to exposure to noise at work.

1) Deadline for implementation of the legislation in the Member States

- 01.01.1990

- 01.01.1991: Greece and Portugal

2) References

Official Journal L 137, 24.05.86

A	ArbeitnehmerInnenschutzgesetz - ASchG	Bundesgesetzblatt N.450/1994, 17/06/94

B	Arrêté Royal du/Koninklijk Besluit van 26/9/91	Moniteur Belge du/Belgisch Staatsblad van 14/11/91

D	Unfallverhütungsvorschriften Lärm (V. Bürgerliches Gesetzbuch 121) 01/01/90	Süddeutsche Eisen- und Stahl-Berufsgenossenschaft

DK	Bekendtgørelse N.319, 17/06/77	Lovtidende A, 17/06/77
	Bekendtgørelse N.392, 10/08/78	Lovtidende A, 10/08/78
	Bekendtgørelse N.32, 29/01/79	Lovtidende A, 29/01/79
	Bekendtgørelse N.43, 22/01/81	Lovtidende A, 22/01/81
	Bekendtgørelse N.323, 07/07/83	Lovtidende A, 07/07/83
	Bekendtgørelse N.452, 27/08/84	Lovtidende A, 27/08/94
	Bekendtgørelse N.646, 18/12/85	Lovtidende A, 18/12/85
	Bekendtgørelse N.490, 21/07/86	Lovtidende A, 21/07/86
	Bekendtgørelse N.889, 28/12/87	Lovtidende A, 28/12/87

E	Real Decreto N.1326/89, 27/10/89	Boletín Oficial del Estado N.263, 02/11/89
	Real Decreto N.1316/89, 27/10/89	Boletín Oficial del Estado N.295, 09/12/89

EL	Décret présidentiel N.85, 05/03/91	Journal Officiel, 18/03/91

F	Décret N.88-405, 21/04/88	Journal Officiel p.5359, 22/04/88
	Décret N.88-930, 20/09/88	Journal Officiel p.12163, 24/09/88
	Arrêté ministériel, 22/04/88	Journal Officiel p.6923, 10/05/88
	Arrêté ministériel, 25/04/88	Journal Officiel p.6465, 07/05/88
	Arrêté ministériel, 31/01/89	Journal Officiel p.1807, 08/02/89
	Circulaire, 06/05/88 du Ministère des Affaires Sociales	
	Normes NF S31-001, S31-025, S31-031, S31-041, S31-048, S31-062, S31-069, S31-081, S31-084, S31-109, S35-005	

FIN	Työturvallisuuslaki (299/58), muutos (144/93) Työterveyshuoltolaki (743/78), 29/09/78 Laki työsusuojelun valvonnasta ja muutoksenhausta työsuojeluasioissa (131/73), uusi nimi (27/87) Valtioneuvosten päätös työntekijäi suojelusta työssä esiintyvän melun aiheuttamilta vaaroilta ja haitoilta (1404/93), 22/12/93 Valtioneuvosten päätös terveystartaskusista erityistä sairastumisen vaaraa aiheuttavissa töissä (1672/92), 30/12/92	

I	Decreto Legislativo N.277, 15/08/91	Gazzetta Ufficiale, 27/08/91, p.3

IRL	S.I.E.C. (Protection of Workers) (Exposure to Noise) Regulations 1990	Statutory Instrument N.157, 1990

L	Règlement Grand Ducal, 26/02/93	Mémorial A, N.31, 21/04/93, p.565

NL	Besluit N.598, 15/11/91	Staatsblad N.598, 1991

P	Decreto-lei N.72/92, 28/04/92 Decreto-lei N.9/92, 28/04/92	Diário da República I Serie A N.98, 28/04/92

S	Arbetsmiljölag Arbetsmiljöförordning	Svensk författningssamling 1977:1160 Svensk författningssamling 1977:1166 Arbetarskyddsstyrelsens författningssamling (AFS) 1992:10

UK	Noise at Work Regulations 1989 Health and Safety at Work Ect Act, 1974 Safety Representatives and Safety Committees Regulations 1977 National Health Service Act, 1977	Statutory Instrument 1989, N.1790 Statutory Instrument 1977, N.500

HEALTH AND SAFETY AT WORK - DANGEROUS AGENTS

Banning of certain specified agents and activities

Council Directive 88/364/EEC of 9 June 1988 on the protection of workers by the banning of certain specified agents and/or certain work activities (fourth individual Directive within the meaning of Article 8 of Directive 80/1107/EEC).

1) Deadline for implementation of the legislation in the Member States

01.01.90

2) References

Official Journal L 179, 09.07.88

A	Arbeitnehmerinnerschutzgesetz	Bundesgesetzblatt N.450/94

B	Arrêté Royal du/Koninklijk Besluit van 17/04/90	Moniteur Belge du/Belgisch Staatsblad van 19/05/90, p.10197

D	Zweite Verordnung zur Änderung der Gefahrstoffverordn. vom 23/04/90	Bundesgesetzblatt Teile 1, II, III), S.790

DK	Bekendtgørelse N.770, 11/12/89	Lovtidende A, 11/12/90

E	Real Decreto N.88/1990, 26/01/90	Boletín Oficial del Estado, 27/01/90

EL	Journal du gouvernement de la Démocratie Hellénique - Athènes	Journal Officiel N.930, Volume B, du 29.12.89

F	Decret N.89-593 du 28/08/89	Journal officiel du 30/08/89, p.10872

FIN	Valtioneuvoston päätös eräitäterveydelle haittaa aiheuttavia kemikaaleja ja niitä sisältäviä tuotteita koskevista kielloistaja rajoituksista (489/92) 27/05/92	Suomen Säädöskokoelma

I	Decreto Legislativo N 77 25/1/92	Gazzetta Ufficiale N 36, 13/2/92

IRL	Factories (Carcinogenic Substance) (Processes) Regulation 1972	Statutory Instrument N.242 of 1972

L	Règlement Grand-Ducal, 02/07/92	Memorial A, N.50, p.1554, 21/07/92

NL	Besluit Specifieke Gezondheidsschadelijke Stoffen Besluit Specifieke Gezondsschadelijke Stoffen van 19/08/91	Staatscourant 1991, 20, 29/01/91 Staatsblad 1991 N.453

P	Decreto-lei N.275/91, 07/08/91	Diário da República I Serie A, N.180, p.3925, 07/08/91

S	Arbetsmiljölag Arbetsmiljöförordning Arbetarskyddstyrelsens kungörelse med föreskrifter om hygieniska gränsvärden Arbetarskyddstyrelsens kungörelse med föreskrifter om hygieniska gränsvärden	Svensk författningssamling 1977:1160 Svensk författningssamling 1977:1166 Arbetarskyddsstyrelsens författningssamling (AFS) 1990:13 Arbetarskyddsstyrelsens författningssamling (AFS) 1993:9

UK	The Control of Substances Hazardous of Health Regulations 1988	Statutory Instrument 1988, N.1657

HEALTH AND SAFETY AT WORK - GENERAL MEASURES

Framework - health and safety at work

Council Directive 89/391/EEC of 12 June 1989 the introduction of measures to encourage improvements in the safety and health of workers at work.

1) Deadline for implementation of the legislation in the Member States

31.12.92

2) References

Official Journal L 183, 29.06.89

A	Heimarbeitsgesetz 1960 in der Fassung des BG BGBl. N. 836/992	Bundesgesetzblatt N.105/61, p.1
	Verordnung des Bundesministers für Arbeit und Soziales über die Fachausbildung der Sicherheitskräfte (SFK-VO)	Bundesgesetzblatt N.277/95, p.3736, 21/04/95
	Bundesbediensteten Schutzgesetz- BSG, 23/03/77	Bundesgesetzblatt N.164/77, p.681, 21/04/77
	Änderung des Bundesbediensteten Schutzgesetzes	Bundesgesetzblatt N.631/94, p.5245, 19/08/94
	Änderung des NÖ Landesbediensteten-schutzgesetzes, 21/02/91	Landesgesetzblatt für das Land Niederösterreich, 24/04/91
	Burgenländisches Landesbedienstetens-chutzgesetz, 17/12/86	Landesgesetzblatt für das Burgenland p.37, 18/03/87
	Kärntner Bedienstetenschutzgesetz, 24/11/80	Landesgesetzblatt 1981, Stück 3, N.5, p.10
	Oberösterreichisches Landesbediebsteten-Schutzgesetz,01/07/81	Landesgesetzblatt für Oberösterreich, p.85, 31/08/81
	Oberösterreichisches Gemeindenbediebsteten-Schutzgesetz,09/03/84	Landesgesetzblatt für Oberösterreich, p.83, 15/06/84
	Landesbediensteten-Schutzgesetz, 11/06/91	Landesgesetzblatt für die Steiermark, p.191, 13/09/91
	Tiroler Bedienstetenschutzgesetz, 13/07/91	Landesgesetzblatt für Tirol, p.215, 13/09/91
	Wiener Bedienstetenschutzgesetz, 26/06/79	
	Gefahrenklassen-Verordnung	Bundesgesetzblatt 637/95, p.7533, 20/09/95
	Verordnung über die Fachausbildung der Sicherheitskräfte (SFK-VO)	Aushangpflichtige Gesetze, Ausgabe August 1995, p.48, 10/08/95
	Verordnung über Einrichtungen in den Betrieben für die Durchführung des Arbeitnehmerschutzes	Aushangpflichtige Gesetze, Ausgabe August 1995, p.51, 10/08/95
	Verordnung über gesundheitliche Eignung von Arbeitnehmern für bestimmte Tätigkeiten	Aushangpflichtige Gesetze, Ausgabe August 1995, p.54, 10/08/95
	Verordnung über den Nachweis der Fachkenntnisse für bestimmte Arbeiten	Aushangpflichtige Gesetze, Ausgabe August 1995, p.58, 10/08/95
	Verordnung über die Betriebsbewilligung nach dem Arbeitnehmerschutzgesetz	Aushangpflichtige Gesetze, Ausgabe August 1995, p.60, 10/08/95
	Verordnung über den Nachweis der Fachkenntnisse für die Vorbereitung und Organisation von Arbeiten unter elekt. Spannung über 1kV	Aushangpflichtige Gesetze, Ausgabe August 1995, p.61, 10/08/95
	Allgemeine Arbeitnehmerschutzverordnung	Aushangpflichtige Gesetze, Ausgabe August 1995, p.63, 10/08/95
	Allgemeine Dienstnehmerschutzverordnung	Aushangpflichtige Gesetze, Ausgabe August 1995, p.99, 10/08/95
	Maschinen-Schutzvorrichtungsverordnung	Aushangpflichtige Gesetze, Ausgabe August 1995, p.108, 10/08/95
	Verordnung über Beschäftigungsverbote und -beschränkungen für weibliche Arbeitnehmer, 29/11/76	Aushangpflichtige Gesetze, Ausgabe August 1995, p.149, 10/08/96
	Verordnung des Bundesministers für Arbeit und Soziales über die Sicherheitsvertrauenspersonen	Bundesgesetzblatt N.172/96, p.6, 12/04/96

(SVP-VO)	
Verordnung über die Fachausbildung der Sicherheitskräfte	
Verordnung über Einrichtungen in den Betrieben für die Durchführung des Arbeitnehmerschutzes	
Verordnung über den Nachweis der Fachkenntnisse für bestimmte Arbeiten	
Verordnung über die Betriebsbewilligung nach dem Arbeitnehmerschutzgesetz	
Allgemeine Arbeitnehmerverordnung Kinder- und Jugendlichenbeschäftigungsgesetz	
Verordnung über Beschäftigungsverbote und beschränkungen für Jugendliche	
Mutterschutzgesetz	
Bundesgesetz über die Nachtarbeit der Frauen	
Verordnung über Beschäftigungsverbote und -beschränkungen für weibliche Arbeitnehmer	
Behinderteneinstellungsgesetz	
Verordnung über arbeitsmed. Zentren (AMZ-VO)	Bundesgesetzblatt 1996, p.3103, 21/08/96
Verordnung über die Sicherheits- und Gesundheitsschutzdokumente (DOK-VO)	Bundesgesetzblatt 1996, p.3261, 10/09/96
Verordnung über die Fachausbildung der Sicherheitskräfte (SFK-VO)	Bundesgesetzblatt 1995, p.3736, 21/04/95
Verordnung über die Geschäftsordnung des Arbeitnehmerschutzbeirates	Bundesgesetzblatt 1997, p.2071, 10/1/97
Verordnung über die Gesundheitsüberwachung am Arbeitsplatz	Bundesgesetzblatt 1997 Teil II N.27 p.89, 30/1/97
Änderung der Verordnung über die Sicherheits und Gesundheitsschutz Dokumente (DOK-VO)	Bungesgesetzblatt 1997 Teil II N.53 p.243, 20/2/97
Bundesgesetz, mit dem das Arbeitnehmer-Innenschutzgesetz, das Arbeitsvertragsrechts-Anpassungs- gesetz und das Mutterschutzgesetz 1979 geändert werden	Bundesgesetzblatt 1997 Teil I N.9 p.35, 10/1/97
Bergpolizeiverordnung über verantwortlmiche Personen-BPV-Personen	Bundesgesetzblatt 1997 Teil II N 108 p.43 24/4/97

B	Arrêté Royal du/Koninklijk Besluit van 14/09/92	Moniteur Belge du/Belgisch Staatsblad van 30/09/92
	Règlement Général/Algemene Verordening, pour la protection au travail	Moniteur Belge du/Belgisch Staatsblad van 08/01/96
	Loi du/Wet van 10/06/52,concernant la santé et la sécurité des travailleurs, ainsi que la salubrité du travail et des lieux de travail	Moniteur Belge du/Belgisch Staatsblad van 19/06/52
	Loi du/Wet van 16/11/72	Moniteur Belge du/Belgisch Staatsblad van 08/12/72
	Loi du/Wet van 16/11/72, betreffende de arbeidinspectie	Moniteur Belge du/Belgisch Staatsblad van 08/12/72
	Loi du/Wet van 03/07/78 betreffende de arbeidsovereen	Moniteur Belge du/Belgisch Staadsblad van 22/08/78
	Loi du/Wet van 28/12/77, tot bescherming van de arbeids geneesheren	Moniteur Belge du/Belgisch Staatsblad van 18/01/78
	Arrêté Royal du/Koninklijk Besluit van 10/08/78	Moniteur Belge du/Belgisch Staatsblad van 03/10/78
	Arrêté Royal du/Koninklijk Besluit van 10/02/79	Moniteur Belge du/Belgisch Staatsblad van 8/3/79
	Arrêté Royal du/Koninklijk Besluit van 11/03/87	Moniteur Belge du/Belgisch Staatsblad van 25/03/87
	Arrêté Royal du/Koninklijk Besluit van 21/04/89	Moniteur Belge du/Belgisch Staatsblad van 10/05/89
	Arrêté Royal du/Koninklijk Besluit van 12/08/94	Moniteur Belge du/Belgisch Staatsblad van 2/8/94
	Arrêté Royal du/Koninklijk Besluit van 12/06/89	Moniteur Belge du/Belgisch Staatsblad N. 20822 van 30/9/92
	Règlement Général/Algemene Verordening, TitreII/Chap.I	Moniteur Belge du/Belgisch Staatsblad van 30/06/83
	Règlement Général/Algemene Verordening 447 Annexes A,22/12/89	Moniteur Belge du/Belgisch Staatsblad van 31/12/89
	Règlement Général/Algemene Verordening 470/24, Annexes A, 22/12/89	Moniteur Belge du/Belgisch Staatsblad van 31/12/89
	Règlement Général/Algemene Verordening 668/677, Annexes B, 03/07/78	Moniteur Belge du/Belgisch Staatsblad van 30/06/85
	Règlement Général/Algemene Verordening 470/37, Annexes A, 22/12/89	Moniteur Belge du/Belgisch Staatsblad van 31/12/89
	Règlement Général/Algemene Verordening 756/155, Annexes E, 30/08/85	Moniteur Belge du/Belgisch Staatsblad van 23/10/85
	Arrêté Royal du/Koninklijk Besluit van 12/01/79	Moniteur Belge du/Belgisch Staatsblad van 8/3/79
	Loi du/Wet van 15/09/19	Moniteur Belge du/Belgisch Staatsblad van 3/3/20
	Arrêté Royal du/Koninklijk Besluit van 12/08/94	Moniteur Belge du/Belgisch Staatsblad van 2/9/94
	Loi du/Wet van 04/08/96 relative au bien-être des travailleurs lors de l'execution de leur travail	Moniteur Belge du/Belgisch Staatsblad van 18/09/96

D	Seemannsgesetz, 26/07/57	Bundesgesetzblatt 1957
	Reichversicherungsordnung Bergverordnungen des Länder Nordrhein-Westfalen, 20/02/70	
	Druckluftverordnung, 04/10/72	Bundesgesetzblatt p.1909, 14/10/72
	Arbeitssicherheltsgesetz, 12/12/73	Bundesgesetzblatt p.1885, 15/12/73
	Bundesbeamtengesetz	
	Beamtenrechtsrahmengesetz	
	Bundespersonalvertretungsgesetz, 15/03/74	Bundesgesetzblatt
	Unfallverhütungsvorschrift VBG 123, 01/04/74	
	Unfallverhütungsvorschrift VBG 122, 01/12/74	
	Unfallverhütungsvorschrift GUV 0.5, 01/03/75	
	Arbeitsstättenverordnung, 20/03/75	Bundesgesetzblatt 1975
	Unfallverhütungsvorschrift (VBG1), 01/04/77	
	Richtlinie, 28/01/78	GMBlatt p.114, 1978
	Bundeslaufbahnverordnung	
	Verordnung, 11/11/77	Bundesgesetzblatt p.2071, 18/11/77
	Unfallverhütungsvorschrift GUV 0.3, 01/05/78	
	Unfallverhütungsvorschrift GUV 01, 01/04/79	
	Unfallverhütungsvorschrift VBG 109, 01/04/79	
	Bundesberggesetz, 13/08/80	Bundesgesetzblatt 1980
	Verordnung, 27/02/80	Bundesgesetzblatt p.173, 01/03/80
	Unfallverhütungsvorschrift UVV see 01/01/81 (UVV 1.1)	
	Unfallverhütungsvorschrift UVV 1.3, 01/01/81	
	Unfallverhütungsvorschrift VBG 103, 01/10/82	
	Unfallverhütungsvorschrift GUV 8.1, 01/09/82	
	Unfallverhütungsvorschrift UVV 1.2, 01/01/85	
	Schwerbehindertengesetz, 26/08/86	Bundesgesetzblatt p.1421, 02/09/86
	Röntgenverordnung, 08/01/87	Bundesgesetzblatt p.114, 14/01/87
	Gewerbeordnung	Bundesgesetzblatt p.426, 29/01/87
	Betriebsverfassungsgesetz, 23/12/88	
	Festlandsockel-Bergverordnung, 21/03/89	Bundesgesetzblatt 1989
	Strahlenschutzverordnung 1889	Bundesgesetzblatt p.1322, 12/07/89
	Chemikaliengesetz, 14/03/90	Bundesgesetzblatt p.521, 22/03/90
	Gentechnik-Sicherheitsverordnung, 24/10/90	Bundesgesetzblatt p.2340, 03/11/90
	Mutterschutzverordnung, 11/01/91	Bundesgesetzblatt p.125, 26/01/91
	Gesundheitsschutz-Bergverordnung, 31/07/91	Bundesgesetzblatt p.1751, 09/08/91
	Störfall-Verordnung, 20/09/91	Bundesgesetzblatt p.1891, 28/09/91
	Unfallverhütungsvorschrift VBG 100, 01/04/93	
	Gefahrstoffverordnung, 26/10/93	Bundesgesetzblatt p.1782, 30/10/93
	Gesetz zur Umsetzung der EG-Rahmenrichtlinie 07/08/96	Bundesgesetzblatt Z 5702, N.43, p.1246, 20/08/96
	Seemannsgesetz 26/07/57	
	Unfallversicherungs-Einordnungsgesetz-UVEG 07/08/96	Bundesgesetzblatt N.43, Teil I, p.1254, 20/08/96
	Rahmenrichtlinie 07/08/96	Bundesgesetzblatt Z.5702, N. 43/96, p.1246, 20/08/96

DK	Bekendtgørelse N.540, 02/09/82 om stoffer og materialer Bekendtgørelse N.469, 06/10/83 om sikkerhedsuddannelse mv. Bekendtgørelse N.646, 18/12/85 Bekendtgørelse N.889, 28/12/87 om bedriftssundhedstjeneste Bekendtgørelse N.235 af 10/04/91 Bekendtgørelse N.746, 28/08/92 om brug af personlige værnemidler Bekendtgørelse N.693, 14/10/91 om byggepladsers og lign. arbejdssteders indretning Søfartsstyrelsens tekniske forskrift N.7, 15/12/92 Bekendtgørelse N.1182, 18/12/92 Bekendtgørelse N.1181, 18/12/92 om virksomhedernes sikkerheds- og sundhedsarbejde Bekendtgørelse af 15/12/92 om anvendelse af tekniske hjælpemidler Bekendtgørelse N.1165 af 16/12/92 om arbejdsmedicinske undersøgelser Bekendtgørelse N.1163, 16/12/92 om faste arbejdssteders indretning Lov N.177, 14/04/93 - arbejdsmiljø Forholdsregler for civil søfart, BL 5-44, 16/06/94	Lovtidende A 1991 Hæfte 52, S.909
E	Decreto-Ley N.31/95, 08/11/95 Orden de 05/03/96 Orden de 16/12/87 Instrucción de la secretaria de Estado para la Administración Pública, 26/02/96 Orden por la que se establecen nuevos modelos para la notificación de accidentes de trabajo y se dan instrucciónes para su cumplimentación y tramitación, 16/12/87 Real decreto 39/1997 de 17/1/97 por el que se aprueba el Reglamento de los Servícios de Prevención	Boletín Oficialdel Estado, p.32590, 10/11/95 Boletín Oficialdel Estado N.59, p.942, 08/03/96 Boletín Oficial del Estado N.311, p.38065, 29/12/87 Boletín Oficial du 08/03/96, p.9421 Boletín Oficial du 29/12/87, p.38065 Boletín Oficial del Estado 17/1/97, p 15

EL	Décret Présidentiel N.149, 14/3/34	Journal Officiel 22/03/34
	Décret Présidentiel N.61, 02/07/75	Journal Officiel p.763, 07/07/75
	Décision A2/ST/1539/85	Journal Officiel p.2769, 13/05/85
	Loi N.1568, 11/10/85	Journal Officiel p.3335, 18/10/85
	Loi N. 1836/89, 14/03/89	Journal Officiel p.1071, 14/03/89
	Décret Présidentiel N.94, 10/04/87	Journal Officiel p.503, 22/04/87
	Décret Présidentiel N.70, 11/02/88	Journal Officiel p.263, 17/02/88
	Loi N.1767, 04/04/88	Journal Officiel p.709, 06/04/88
	Décret Présidentiel N.294, 17/6/88	Journal Officiel p.2781, 21/06/88
	Loi N.1837, 03/89	Journal Officiel p.1105, 23/03/89
	Décret Présidentiel N.368/89	Journal Officiel p.3917, 16/06/89
	Décret Présidentiel N.369/89	Journal Officiel p.3981, 16/06/89
	Décision N.13062, 07/03/90	Journal Officiel p.187, 08/03/90
	Décret Présidentiel N.85, 05/03/91	Journal Officiel p.619, 18/03/91
	Décret Présidentiel N.436 16/10/91	Journal Officiel p.2125, 24/10/91
	Loi N.22224, 05/07/94	Journal Officiel p.1469, 06/07/94
	Décret ministérielle N.17, du 18/01/96	Journal Officiel du Gouvernement N.11, Volume I, p.93, 18/01/96

F	Décret N.82-453, 28/05/82	
	Décret N.85-755, 19/07/85	
	Loi N.91-1414, 31/12/91	Journal Officiel, 07/01/92
	Décision N.92-158, 31/12/91	Journal Officiel, 22/02/92, p.2779
	Décret N.92-158, 20/02/92	Journal Officiel, 22/02/92, p.2779
	Décret N.92-333, 31/03/92	Journal Officiel, 01/04/92, p.4614

FIN	Lag om skydd i arbete 58/299, 28/06/58	
	Lag om arbete inom företag 78/725, 22/09/78	
	Lag om arbetsavtal 70/320,30/04/70	
	Lag om företagshälsovård 78/743, 29/09/78	
	Förordning om tillsynen över arbetarskyddet 73/954, 21/12/73	
	Laki Rikoslain muuttamiseta, 21/04/95	
	Vahingonkorvaauslaki, 31/05/74	
	Kuntalaki, 17/03/95	
	Sisaeasiainministeriön maeaeraeyskokoelma 18/91, 30/10/91	
	Yleissopimus yhteistoimintamenettelystae solveltamisohjeineen, 24/05/93	
	Asetus työturvallisuuslain ja työterveyshuoltolain soveltamisesta työturvallisuuslain §2: ssae tarkoitettuun työhön, 27/05/88	

	Valtion virkamieslaki, 19/08/94 Valtioneuvosten paeaetös terveystarkastuksista erityistae sairastumisen vaaraa aiheuttavissa töissae, 30/12/92 Sisaeasiainministeriön maeaeraeys 7/94, 19/12/94 Valtioneuvosten paeaetös alusten lastauksessa ja purkamisessa kaeytettaevistae jaerjestysohjeista, 28/11/85	

I	Decreto legislativo N.626, 19/09/94 Decreto legislativo N.242, 19/03/96	Supplemento Ordinario alla Gazzetta Ufficiale p.3, N.141, 12/11/94 Gazzetta Ufficiale p.5, 06/05/96

IRL	The Safety Health and Welfare at Work (Generales applications) 1993	Statutory Instrument N.44, 1993

L	Loi du 08/06/94 Loi du 17/06/94 Loi du 17/06/94	Mémorial A N.55, p.1050, 01/07/94 Mémorial A N.55, p.1054, 01/07/94 Mémorial p.1060, 01/07/94

NL	Arbeidsomstandighedenwet Besluit Arbodiensten van 28/12/93 Besluit Bedrijfshulpverlening Arbeidsomstandighedenwet, 28/12/93 Ministeriële Regeling Certificatie Arbodiensten van 28/12/93 Deskundigheidseisen Arbodiensten van 28/12/93 Besluit Arveidsomstandighedenwet	Staatsblad N.757 Staatsblad N.782 Staatscourant N.252, 30/12/93, Blz.38 Blz.38 Staatsblad N.782

P	Declaracao Rectificacao N.65/91, 30/04/91 Decreto-lei N.441/91, 14/11/91 Decreto-lei N.26/94, 01/02/94	Diário da República I Serie A. N.99, p.2380 (2), 30/04/91 Diário da República I Serie A. N.262, p.5826, 14/11/91 Diário da República I Serie A. N.26, p.480, 01/02/94

S	AFS 84:14 Första hjälpen, 20/09/84	Arbetarskyddsstyrelens Författningssamling, 02/11/84
	AFS 93:56 Utrymning 25/11/93 AFS 92:6 Internkontroll av Arbetsmiljön, 21/05/92 Arbetsmiljölag 77:1160, 19/12/77 Arbetsmiljöförordning 77:1166, 19/12/77	Arbetarskyddsstyrelens Författningssamling, 29/06/92

UK	The Health and Safety at Work etc. Act 1974	
	Industrial Relations Order 1976	Statutory Rules of Northern Ireland N.1043 (N.I. 16) of 1976
	Safety Representatives and Safety Commitees Regulations 1977	Statutory Instrument N.500, 1977
	The Health and Safety at Work (Northern Ireland) Order 1978	Statutory Instrument N.1039, 1978
	Employment Protection (consolidation) act 1978	
	Safety Representatives and Safety Committeees Regulations, 1979	Statutory Rules of Northern Ireland N.437 of 1979
	The Health and Safety (First-Aid) Regulations 1981 of 29/06/81	Statutory Instrument N.917, 1981
	The Reporting of Injuries,	Statutory Instrument N.2023, 1985
	Health and Safety (First-Aid) Regu. (Northern Ireland) 1982	Statutory Rules of Norhern Ireland N.429 of 1982
	Fire Service Order 1984	Statutory Rules of Northern Ireland N.1821 (N.I. 11) of 1984
	Diseases and Dangerous Occurences Regulations 1985 of 17/12/85	
	The Relevant Statutory Provision for Northern Ireland Reporting of Injuries, diseases and Dangerous occurences Regulations	Statutory Rules of Northern Ireland N.247 of 1986
	The Management of Health and Safety at Work Regulations 1992	Statutory Instrument N.2051, 1992
	The Personal Protective Equipment at Work Regulations, 25/11/92	Statutory Instrument N.2966, 1992
	Management of Health and Saftey at Work Regulations 1992	Statutory Rules of Northern Ireland N.459 of 1992
	Employment Rights Act 1993	
	Personal Protective Equipment at Work Regulations, 1993	Statutory Rules of Northern Ireland N.20 of 1993
	The Health and Safety(consultation with employees) Regulations 1996, 10/06/96	Statutory Instrument N.1513, p.1,
	Factories ordinance, Factories (safety) Regulations 1996, 25/01/96	Second supplement to the Gibraltar Gazette N.2894, p.149, 25/01/96
	Fire precautions (workplace) Regulations, 28/7/97	Statutory Instruments 1997 N 1840 p.1

HEALTH AND SAFETY AT WORK - THE WORKPLACE AND CATEGORIES OF WORKERS PARTICULARLY AT RISK

Minimum safety and health requirements for the workplace

Council Directive 89/654/EEC of 30 November 1989 concerning the minimum safety and health requirements for the workplace (first individual Directive within the meaning of Article 16(1) of Directive 89/391/EEC).

1) Deadline for implementation of the legislation in the Member States

- 31.12.1992

- 31.12.1994: Greece.

2) References

Official Journal L 393, 30.12.1989

A	Bundesgesetz über Sicherheit und Gesundheitsschutz bei der Arbeit Allgemeine Arbeitnehmerschutzver-ordnung Allgemeine Dienstnehmerschutzver-ordnung	Bundesgesetzblatt, S. 3785, 17/06/94
	Elektroschutzverordnung 1995-ESV 1995 Betrieb von Starkstromanlagen - grundsätzliche Bestimmungen	Bundesgesetzblatt S 237 p.8381, 25/10/95 Österreichische Bestimmungen für die Elektrotechnik ÖVE-E-5, Teil 1/1989, N 47 p.696 20/1/94
	Sonderbestimmungen für den Betrieb elektrischer Anlagen in explosionsgefährdeten Betriebstätten	Österreichische Bestimmungen für die Elektrotechnik ÖVE-E-5, Teil 9/1982, N 47 p.721 20/1/94
	Betrieb elektrischer Bahnanlagen	Österreichische Bestimmungen für die Elektrotechnik ÖVE-T 5/1990, p.1770, 20/1/94
	Errichtung von Starkstromanlagen mit Nennpannungen bis 1000 V und 1500 V	Österreichische Bestimmungen für die Elektrotechnik ÖVE-EN 1, Teil 1/1989, p.913 20/1/94
	Nachtrag A zu den Bestimmungen über Errichtung von Starkstromanlagen bis 1000 V und 1500 V	Österreichische Bestimmungen für die Elektrotechnik ÖVE-EN 1, Teil 3/1986, p.1031 20/1/94
	Nachtrag A und Nachtrag B zu den Bestimmungen über Errichtung von	Österreichische Bestimmungen für die Elektrotechnik ÖVE-EN 1, Teil 3/1985, p.1052

	Starkstromanlagen mit Nennspannungen bis 1000 V und 1500 V	20/1/94
	Errichtung von Starkstromanlagen mit Nennpannungen bis 1000 V und 1500 V Teil 4: Anlagen besonderer Art	Österreichische Bestimmungen für die Elektrotechnik ÖVE-EN 1, Teil 4/1980, p.1063 20/1/94
	Errichtung von Starkstromanlagen mit Nennpannungen bis 1000 V und 1500 V Teil 4: besondere Anlagen	Österreichische Bestimmungen für die Elektrotechnik ÖVE-EN 1, Teil 4, p.1078 20/1/94
	Errichtung von elektrischer Anlagen in explosionsgefährdeten Bereichen	Österreichische Bestimmungen für die Elektrotechnik ÖVE-EX 65/1981, p.1276, 20/1/94
	Nachtrag A zu den Bestimmungen über die Errichtung elektrischer Anlagen in explosionsgefährdeten Bereichen	Österreichische Bestimmungen für die Elektrotechnik ÖVE-EX 65a/1985, p.1303 20/1/94
	Errichtung von Starkstromanlagen mit Nennspannung über 1 kV	Österreichische Bestimmungen für die Elektrotechnik ÖVE-EH 1/1982, p.823, 20/1/94
	Nachtrag A zu den Bestimmungen über die Errichtung von Starkstromanlagen mit Nennspannung über 1 kV	Österreichische Bestimmungen für die Elektrotechnik ÖVE-EH 1a/1987, p.861, 20/1/94

B	Arrêté Royal du/Koninklijk Besluit van 18/06/93	Moniteur Belge du/Belgisch Staatsblad van 08/07/93

D	Bauordnungen des Länder (p.e. Bayerische Bauordnung, Landesbau-ordnung für Baden-Württemberg, Bauordnung für das Land Nordrhein-Westfalen) Bay 2/7/82, BW 28/11/83, NW 26/06/84)	
	Druckluftverordnung, 04/10/72	Bundesgesetzblatt p.1909, 14/10/72
	Arbeitsstättenverordnung, 20/03/75	Bundesgesetzblatt 1975
	Unfallverhütungsvorschrift (VBG1), 01/04/77	
	Unfallverhütungsvorschrift, (VBG 37), 01/04/77	
	Unfallverhütungsvorschrift, (GUV 0.3), 01/05/78	
	Unfallverhütungsvorschrift, (VBG 55a), 01/08/78	
	Unfallverhütungsvorschrift GUV2.10, 01/12/78	
	Unfallverhütungsvorschrift UVV 1.4	
	Unfallverhütungsvorschrift VBG 4, 01/04/79	
	Unfallverhütungsvorschrift, (VBG 109), 01/04/79	
	Verordnung, 27/02/80	Bundesgesetzblatt p.173, 01/03/80
	Unfallverhütungsvorschrift UVV see 01/01/81 (UVV 1.1)	
	Unfallverhütungsvorschrift UVV 2.1 01/01/81	
	Unfallverhütungsvorschrift, (UVV 1.3), 01/01/81	
	Unfallverhütungsvorschrift, (VBG 72), 01/10/85	

	Schwerbehindertengesetz 26/08/86	Bundesgesetzblatt p.1421, 02/09/86
	Gewerbeordnung	Bundesgesetzblatt p.426, 29/01/87
	Unfallverhütungsvorschrift, (VBG 20), 01/04/87	
	(VBG 23 und VBG 50), 01/04/88, (GUV 7.4),	
	01/09/88	
	Unfallverhütungsvorschrift, (VBG 125), 01/04/89	
	Mutterschutzgesetz	Bundesgesetzblatt
	Gefahrstoffverordnung, 26/10/93	Bundesgesetzblatt p.1782, 30/10/93

DK	Bekendtgørelse N.505, 19/11/80 om sikkerhedsskiltning	
	Lov N.646, 18/12/85 m. senere ændr	
	Bekendtgørelse N.694 af 07/08/92	
	om indretning af tekn. hjælpemidl.	
	Bekendtgørelse N.746, 28/08/92 om brug af personlige værnemidler	
	Bekendgørelse N.1163, 16/12/92 om faste arbejdssteders indretning	
	Bekendtgørelse N.1181, 18/12/92 om arbejdets udførelse	
	Bekendtgørelse N.1182 af 18/12/92 om virksomhedernes sikkerheds- og sundhedsarbejde	
	Bekendtgørelse, 18/12/92 om anvendelse af tekniske hjælpemidler	
	Lov N.177, 14/04/93 - arbejdsmiljø	

E	Ordenanza General de Seguridad e Higiene en el trabajo	
	Orden 31/10/73 - Instrucciónes complementarias del Reglamento Electrotécnico para Baja Tensión	Boletín Oficial del Estado p.4031, 31/12/73
	Orden 30/09/80 - Normas UNE de obligado cumplimiento en la Instrucción MI.BT.044 complementaria del Reglamento Electrotécnico para Baja Tensión	Boletín Oficial del Estado p.2941, 17/10/80
	Orden 24/07/92 - Modifia la Instrucción técnica complementaria MI.BT.026 del Reglamento Electrotécnico para Baja Tensión	Boletín Oficial del Estado p.4624, 04/08/92
	Orden 19/12/77 - Modifia la Instrucción complementaria MI.BT.025 del Reglamento Electrotécnico para Baja Tensión	Boletín Oficial del Estado p.81, 13/01/78
	Orden 19/12/77 - Modifia Instrucciónes complementaria MI.BT.004,007 y 017 del Reglamento Electrotécnico para Baja Tensión	Boletín Oficial del Estado p.191, 26/01/78
	Orden 28/07/80 - Modifia Instrucción	Boletín Oficial del Estado p.2449, 13/08/80

complementaria MI.BT.040 del Reglamento Electrotécnico para Baja Tensión	
Decreto N.2413/73, 20/09/73, Reglamento Electrotécnico para Baja Tensión	Boletín Oficial del Estado p.3117, 09/10/73
Decreto N.3151/68, 28/11/68, Reglamento de líneas aéras de alta tensión	Boletín Oficial del Estado p.2200, 27/12/68
Real Decreto N.1942/93, 05/11/93, Reglamento de instalaciones de protección	Boletín Oficial del Estado p.12894, 14/12/93
Real Decreto N.279/91, 01/03/91	Boletín Oficial del Estado p.1576, 08/03/91
Orden 11/07/83 - Modifia la Instrucción técnica complementaria MI.BT.008 del Reglamento Electrotécnico para Baja Tensión y declara de obligado cumplimiento diversas normas UNE	Boletín Oficial del Estado p.2434, 22/07/83
Real Decreto 486/1997, de 14/4/97 por el que se establecen las disposiciones mínimas de seguridad y salud en los lugares de trabajo	Boletín Oficial del Estado p 9, 23/4/97

EL	Décret Présidentiel N.149, 14/3/34	22/03/34
	Loi N. 1568/85, 11/10/85	Journal Officiel p.3335, 18/10/85
	Décret Présidentiel N.16, 18/01/96	Journal Officiel Volume A, p.77, 18/01/96

F	Décret N.92-322, 31/03/92	Journal Officiel, 01/04/92
	Décret N.92-323, 31/03/92	
	Arrêté, 04/11/93	Journal Officiel N.17581, 17/12/93
	Décret N.92-332, 31/03/92	Journal Officiel, 01/04/92
	Décret N.92-332, 31/03/92	Journal Officiel, N.4614, 01/04/92
	Loi N. 91-1414 du 31/12/91	Journal Officiel, 01/01/92
	Loi N. 91-1414 du 31/12/91	Journal Officiel, p.319, 07/01/92

FIN	Työturvallisuuslaki 58/299, 28/06/58	
	Rakennuslaki 58/370, 16/08/58	
	Rakennusasetus 59/266, 26/06/59	

I	Decreto Legislativo N.626, 19/09/94	Supplemento Ordinario alla Gazzetta Ufficiale N.141, p.3, 12/11/94

IRL	The Safety, Health and Welfare at Work (General Application) Regulations 1993	Statutory Instruments N.44 of 1993

L	Règlement Grand Ducal 04/11/94	Mémorial A N.96, p.1816, 17/11/94
NL	Besluit Arbeidsplaatsen, 08/10/93	Staatsblad N.534
P	Decreto-lei N.347/93, 01/10/93 Portaria N.987/93, 06/10/93	Diário da República I Serie A, N.231, 01/10/93 Diário da República I Serie B, N.234, 06/10/93
S	Arbetsmiljög 1977:1160, 19/12/77 Arbetsmiljöförordning 1977:1166, 19/12/77 Plan-och bygglag 1987:10, 08/01/87 Lag innefattande vissa bestämmelser om elektriska anläggningar 1902:71, 27/06/02 Förordning om elektrisk materiel 1989:420, 01/06/89 Räddningstjänstlag 1989:1102, 11/12/86 Kungörelse om åtgärder mot Luftföroreningar AFS 1980:11, 19/08/80 Kungörelse om skydddsåtgärder mot skada genom fall AFS 1981:14, 20/08/81 Kungörelse om skydddsåtgärder mot skada ras 20/08/81 Kungörelse om arbetsställningar och arbetsrörelser 25/03/83 Kungörelse om takarbete, 21/04/83 Kungörelse med föreskrifter om första hjälpen vid olycksfall och akut sjukdom, 20/09/84 Kungörelse med föreskrifter om rulltrappor och rullrämper, 24/10/86 Kungörelse med föreskrifter om vissa arbeten på fartyg, 05/12/86 Kungörelse med föreskrifter om belysning, 12/12/91, Kungörelse med föreskrifter om personalutrymmen 19/03/92	Arbetarskyddstyrelsens författningssamling p.3, 11/09/80 Arbetarskyddstyrelsens författningssamling p.3, 14/09/81 AFS 1981:15, AFS 1983:6, p.3, 11/05/83 AFS 1983:12, p.3, 15/07/83 AFS 1984:14, p.3, 02/11/84 AFS 1986:16, p.3, 22/12/86 AFS 1986:26, p.3, 10/02/87 AFS 1991:8, p.3, 14/12/91 AFS p.5, 22/05/92

	Kungörelse med föreskrifter om buller, 21/05/92	AFS 1992:10, p.5, 11/09/92
	Kungörelse med föreskrifter om varselmärkning på arbetsplatser, 20/08/92	AFS 1992:15, p.5, 19/10/92
	Kungörelse med föreskrifter om ventilation och luftkvalitet I arbetslokaler, 29/04/93	AFS 1993:5, p.5, 02/08/93
	Kungörelse med föreskrifter om maskiner och vissa andra tekniska anordningar, 19/08/93	AFS p.9, 05/10/93

UK	The Safety Representatives and Health and Safety Work etc. Act 1977	Statutory Instruments N.500 of 1977
	The Health and Safety at Work (Northern Ireland) of 25/07/78	Statutory Instruments N.1039 of 1978
	Safety Representatives and Safety Committees Regulations (Northern Ireland) of 12/12/79	Statutory Rules of Northern Ireland, N.437, 1979
	The Health and Safety (First-Aid) Regulations of 29/06/81	Statutory Instruments N.917 of 1981
	Health and Safety Regulations 1982	Statutory Rules of Northern Ireland N.429, 1982
	The Fire Services (Northern Ireland) Order of 22/11/84	Statutory Instruments N.1821 of 1984
	The Control of Substances Hazardous to Health Regulations of 26/08/88	Statutory Instruments N.1657 of 1988
	The Noise at Work Regulations of 02/10/89	Statutory Instruments N.1790 of 1989
	The Electricity at Work Regulations of 07/04/89	Statutory Instruments N.635 of 1989
	Building Regulations (Northern Ireland) of 1990	Statutory Rules of Northern Ireland N.59, 1990
	Noise at Work Regulations of 1990	Statutory Rules of Northern Ireland N.147, 1990
	Control of Substances Hazardous to Health Regulations, 11/10/90	Statutory Rules of Northern Ireland N.374, 1990
	The Building Standards (Scotland) Regulations of 01/11/90	Statutory Instruments N.2179 of 1990
	Electricity at Work Regulations (Northern Ireland) of 14/01/91	Statutory Rules of Northern Ireland N.13, 1991
	Building (Amendment) Regulations Northern Ireland of 22/04/91	Statutory Rules of Northern Ireland N.169, 1991
	The Building Regulations of 06/12/91	Statutory Instruments N.2768 of 1991
	The Management of Health and Safety at Work Regulations 1992	Statutory Instruments N.2051 of 1992
	The Workplace (Health Safety and Welfare) Regulations 1992	Statutory Instruments N.3004 of 1992
	Management of Health and Safety at Work Regulations (Northern Ireland) of 26/10/92	Statutory Rules of Northern Ireland N.459, 1992
	Workplace (Health, Safety and Welfare) Regulations 03/02/93	Statutory Rules of Northern Ireland N.37 of 1993
	Fire precautions (workplace) Regulations 1997 28/7/97	Statutory Instruments 1997 N 1840 p.1

HEALTH AND SAFETY AT WORK - THE WORKPLACE AND CATEGORIES OF WORKERS PARTICULARLY AT RISK

Use of work equipment

Council Directive 89/655/EEC of 30 November 1989 concerning the minimum safety and health requirements for the use of work equipment by workers at work (second individual Directive within the meaning of Article 16(1) of Directive 89/391/EEC).

Council Directive 95/63/EC of 5 December 1995 amending Council Directive 89/655/EEC concerning the minimum safety and health requirements for the use of work equipment by workers at work (second individual Directive within the meaning of Article 16(1) of Directive 89/391/EEC).

1) Deadline for implementation of the legislation in the Member States

Directive 89/655/EEC: 31.12.1992

Directive 95/63/EC: 04.12.1998

2) References

Official Journal L 393, 30.12.1989

Official Journal L 335, 30.12.1995

A	Bundesgesetz über Sicherheit und Gesundheitsschutz bei der Arbeit Allgemeine Arbeitnehmerschutzver-ordnung Allgemeine Dienstnehmerschutzver-ordnung Maschinen Schutzvorrichtungsver-ordnung	Bundesgesetzblatt, S. 3785, 17/06/94
	Aufzüge-Sicherheitsverordnung 1996 - ASV 1996 Verordnung des Bundesministers für wirtschaftliche Angelegenheiten und des Bundesministers für Arbeit und Soziales über die Sicherheit von Aufzügen	Bundesgesetzblatt N; 780/96, 30/12/96 Bundesgesetzblatt für die Republik Österreich Nr.780/96, 30/12/96
	Elektroschutzverordnung 1995-ESV 1995 Betrieb von Starkstromanlagen - grundsätzliche Bestimmungen	Bundesgesetzblatt S 237 p.8381, 25/10/95 Österreichische Bestimmungen für die Elektrotechnik ÖVE-E-5, Teil 1/1989, N 47 p.696 20/1/94

	Sonderbestimmungen für den Betrieb elektrischer Anlagen in explosionsgefährdeten Betriebstätten	Österreichische Bestimmungen für die Elektrotechnik ÖVE-E-5, Teil 9/1982, N 47 p.721 20/1/94
	Betrieb elektrischer Bahnanlagen	Österreichische Bestimmungen für die Elektrotechnik ÖVE-T 5/1990, p.1770, 20/1/94
	Errichtung von Starkstromanlagen mit Nennpannungen bis 1000 V und 1500 V	Österreichische Bestimmungen für die Elektrotechnik ÖVE-EN 1, Teil 1/1989, p.913 20/1/94
	Nachtrag A zu den Bestimmungen über Errichtung von Starkstromanlagen bis 1000 V und 1500 V	Österreichische Bestimmungen für die Elektrotechnik ÖVE-EN 1, Teil 3/1986, p.1031 20/1/94
	Nachtrag A und Nachtrag B zu den Bestimmungen über Errichtung von Starkstromanlagen mit Nennspannungen bis 1000 V und 1500 V	Österreichische Bestimmungen für die Elektrotechnik ÖVE-EN 1, Teil 3/1985, p.1052 20/1/94
	Errichtung von Starkstromanlagen mit Nennpannungen bis 1000 V und 1500 V Teil 4: Anlagen besonderer Art	Österreichische Bestimmungen für die Elektrotechnik ÖVE-EN 1, Teil 4/1980, p.1063 20/1/94
	Errichtung von Starkstromanlagen mit Nennpannungen bis 1000 V und 1500 V Teil 4: besondere Anlagen	Österreichische Bestimmungen für die Elektrotechnik ÖVE-EN 1, Teil 4, p.1078 20/1/94
	Errichtung von elektrischer Anlagen in explosionsgefährdeten Bereichen	Österreichische Bestimmungen für die Elektrotechnik ÖVE-EX 65/1981, p.1276, 20/1/94
	Nachtrag A zu den Bestimmungen über die Errichtung elektrischer Anlagen in explosionsgefährdeten Bereichen	Österreichische Bestimmungen für die Elektrotechnik ÖVE-EX 65a/1985, p.1303 20/1/94
	Errichtung von Starkstromanlagen mit Nennspannung über 1 kV	Österreichische Bestimmungen für die Elektrotechnik ÖVE-EH 1/1982, p.823, 20/1/94
	Nachtrag A zu den Bestimmungen über die Errichtung von Starkstromanlagen mit Nennspannung über 1 kV	Österreichische Bestimmungen für die Elektrotechnik ÖVE-EH 1a/1987, p.861, 20/1/94

B	Arrêté Royal du/Koninklijk Besluit van 12/08/93 concernant l'utilisation des équipements de travail	Moniteur Belge du/Belgisch Staatsblad van 28/09/93

D	Bergverordnungen des Länder Nordrhein-Westfalen, 20/02/70 Druckluftverordnung, 04/10/72 Bauordnungen des Länder (Bayerische Bauordnung, Landesbauordnung für Baden-Württemberg, Bauordnung für das Land Nordrhein-Westfalen), Bay 02/07/82, BW 28/11/83, NW 26/06/84	Bundesgesetzblatt p.1909, 14/10/72 Bundesgesetzblatt

	Verordnung, 17/12/74	Bundesgesetzblatt p.3591, 20/12/74
	Unfallverhütungsvorschrift (VBG1), 01/04/77	
	Unfallverhütungsvorschrift (VBG 2)	
	Unfallverhütungsvorschrift VBG55a, 01/08/78	
	Unfallverhütungsvorschrift GUV 01, 01/04/79	
	Unfallverhütungsvorschrift VBG55a, 01/08/78	
	Aufzugsverordnung, 27/02/80	Bundesgesetzblatt
	Verordnung, 27/02/80	Bundesgesetzblatt p.173, 01/03/80
	Unfallverhütungsvorschrift UVV see 01/01/81 (UVV 1.1)	
	Unfallverhütungsvorschrift UVV 3.1, 01/01/81	
	Unfallverhütungsvorschrift UVV 3.2, 01/01/81	
	Unfallverhütungsvorschrift VBG 5, 01/10/85	
	Gewerbeordnung	Bundesgesetzblatt p.426, 29/01/87
	Festlandsockel-Bergverordnung, 21/03/89	Bundesgesetzblatt 1989
	Druckbehälterverordnung 21/04/89	Bundesgesetzblatt p.843, 27/04/89
	Unfallverhütungsvorschrift VBG 12, 01/10/90	
	Störfall-Verordnung, 20/09/91	Bundesgesetzblatt p.1891, 28/09/91
	Unfallverhütungsvorschrift VBG 3, 01/04/92	
	Gefahrstoffverordnung, 26/10/93	Bundesgesetzblatt p.1782, 30/10/93
	Arbeitsmittelbenutzungsverordnung AMBV 11/3/97	Bundesgesetzblatt 1997 Teil II N.16, 19/3/97

DK	Lov N.292, 10/06/81 - havneanlæg	
	Bekendgørelse N.646, 18/12/85 med senere ændringer	
	Bekendtgørelse N.711, 16/11/87 om sikkerhed mv. på havneanlæg Søfartsstyrelsens tekniske for-skrift N.7, 15/12/92	
	Bekendtgørelse N.1163, 16/12/92 om faste arbejdspladsers indretning	
	Bekendtgørelse N.1181, 18/12/92	
	Bekendtgørelse N.1182, 18/12/92 om virksomhedernes sikkerheds- og sundhedsarbejde	
	Bekendtgørelse, 15/12/92 om anv. af tekniske hjælpemidler	
	Lov N.177, 14/04/93 - arbejdsmiljø	
	Bekendtgørelse N.912, 19/11/92 om anvendelse af tekniske hjælpemidl. på havneanlæg	

E	Real Decreto 1215/1997 por el que se establecen les disposiciones mínimas de seguridad y salud para la utilización por los trabajadores de los equipos de trabajo, 18/7/97	Boletín oficial del Estado N 188, p.24063 7/8/97

EL	Décret Présidentiel N.149, 14/3/34	22/03/34
	Décret Royal, 17/09/34	Journal Officiel, 04/10/34
	Décret Royal N.362/68, 18/05/68	Journal Officiel, 27/05/68
	Décret Royal N.464/68, 28/06/68	Journal Officiel, 12/07/68
	Décret Présidentiel N.151/78, 22/02/78	Journal Officiel p.250, 25/02/78
	Décret Présidentiel N.152/78, 22/02/78	Journal Officiel p.252, 25/02/78
	Décret Présidentiel N.1073/81, 12/09/81	Journal Officiel p.3611, 16/09/81
	Loi N. 1568/85, 11/10/85	Journal Officiel p.3335, 18/10/85
	Loi N. 1836/89, 14/03/89	Journal Officiel p.1071, 14/03/89
	Décret Présidentiel N.395/94, 17/12/94	Journal Officiel p.3973, 19/12/94

F	Loi N.91-1414, 31/12/91	Journal Officiel, 07/01/92
	Loi N.91-1414, 31/12/91	Journal Officiel N.319/92
	Décret N. 93-41, 11/01/93	Journal Officiel 13/01/93
	Arrêté, 04/05/93	
	Arrêté, 09/05/93	
	Décret N. 93-40, 11/01/93	Journal Officiel 13/01/93
	Arrêté, 05/05/93	

FIN	Työturvallisuuslaki 58/299, 28/06/58, muutos 93/144	
	Työterveyshuoltolaki 78/743, 29/09/78	
	Laki työsuojelun valvonnasta ja muutoksenhausta työsuojeluasioissa 73/131 16/02/73, uusi nimi 29/87	
	Statsrådets beslut om trygg användning av arbetsutrustning 33/1403, 22/12/93	Finlands Författningssamling p.3659, 28/12/93

I	Decreto Legislativo N.626, 19/09/94	Supplemento Ordinario alla Gazzetta Ufficiale N.141 p.3, 12/11/94

IRL	The Safety, Health and Welfare at Work (General Application) Regulations 1993	Statutory Instruments N.44 of 1993

L	Règlement Grand Ducal 04/11/94 Règlement Grand Ducal modifiant le RGD du 4/11/94, 17/8/97	Mémorial A N.96, p.1826, 17/11/94 Mémorial - JO du Grand-Duché de Luxembourg p.2073, 5/9/97

NL	Besluit van 14/10/93	Staatsblad N.537, 1993 Blz.1

P	Decreto-lei N.331/93, 25/09/93	Diário da República I Serie A, p.5393, 25/09/93

S	Arbetsmiljölag 1977:1160, 19/12/77 Arbetsmiljöförordning 1977:1166, 19/12/77 Kungörelse med föreskrifter om anvaendning av arbetsutrustning, 28/10/93 Kungörelse om arbetslokaler Kungörelse om användning av arbetsutrustning	 AFS 1993:36, p.5, 13/12/93 AFS 1995:3 11/9/95 AFS 1996:5 29/11/96

UK	The Health and Safety at Work Etc. Act 1974	
	The Safety Representatives and Safety Committees Regulations 1977	Statutory Instrument N.500 of 1977
	The Health and Safety at Work (N.I.) Order 1978 of 25/07/78	Statutory Rules of Northern Ireland, N.9
	The Safety Representatives and Safety Committees Regulations (N.I.) 1979 of 12/12/79	Statutory Rules of Northern Ireland 1979,p.437
	The Control of Lead at Work Regulations 1980	Statutory Instrument N.1248 of 1980
	The Ionising Radations Regulations 1985	Statutory Instrument N.2966 of 1992 and Statutory Instrument N.3068, 1992
	The Ionising Radiations Regulations 1985 of 14/10/85	Statutory Rules of Northern Ireland 1985, N.273
	The Ionising Radations Regulatiojns 1985	Statutory Instruments N.1333 of 1985
	The Ionising Radations Regulations 1985	Amended by Statutory Instrument N.2966, 1992
	The Control of Lead at Work Regulations 1986 of 31/01/86	Statutory Rules of Northern Ireland1986, N.36
	The Control of Asbetos at Work Regulations 1987	Statutory Instruments NO 2115 of 1987
	The Control of Substances hazardous to Health Regulations, 1988	Statutory Instruments N.1657 of 1988
	The Control of Asbestos at Work Regu. (N.I.) 1988 of 08/03/88	Statutory Rules of Northern Ireland 1988, N.74 Amended by Statutory Instrument N.2026 of 1990, by Statutory Instrument N.2431 of 1991, by Statutory Instrument N.2382 of 1992 and by N.2966 of 1992
	The Management of Health and Safety at Work Regulations 1992	Statutory Instruments N.2051 of 1992
	The Provision and Use of Work Equipment Regulations 1992	Statutory Instruments N.2932 of 1992
	The Electricity at Work Regu. 1989 of 07/04/89	Statutory Instrument N.635, 1989
	The Control of Substances Hazardous to Health Regulations (N.I.) 1990 of 11/10/90	Statutory Rules of N.I. N.374, 1990, Amended by Statutory Rules of N.I. 61 of 1992
	The Electricity at Work Regu. (N.I.) 1991	Statutory Rules of Northern Ireland 1991, N.13
	The Management of Health and Safety at Work Regulations (N.I.) 1992 of 26/10/92	Statutory Rules of Northern Ireland 1992, N.459
	The Provision and Use of Work Equipment Regulations 1993	Statutory Rules of N.I. N.19 of 1993

HEALTH AND SAFETY AT WORK - THE WORKPLACE AND CATEGORIES OF WORKERS PARTICULARLY AT RISK

Use of personal protective equipment

Council Directive 89/656/EEC of 30 November 1989 on the minimum health and safety requirements for the use by workers of personal protective equipment at the workplace (third individual Directive within the meaning of Article 16(1) of Directive 89/391/EEC).

1) Deadline for implementation of the legislation in the Member States

31.12.92

2) References

Official Journal L 393, 30.12.89

A	Bundesgesetz über Sicherheit und Gesundheitsschutz bei der Arbeit Allgemeine Arbeitnehmerschutzverordnung Allgemeine Dienstnehmerschutzverordnung	Bundesgesetzblatt, S. 3785, 17/06/94
B	Arrêté Royal du/Koninklijk Besluit van 07/08/95	Moniteur Belge du/Belgisch Staatsblad van 15/09/95
D	Bergverordnungen des Länder Nordrhein-Westfalen, 20/02/70 Druckluftverordnung, 04/10/72 Bauordnungen des Länder (Baye-ris che Bauordnung, Landesbauordnung für Baden-Württemberg, Bauordnung für das Land Nordrhein-Westfalen), Bay 02/07/82, BW 28/11/83, NW 26/06/84 Reichversicherungsordnung	Bundesgesetzblatt p.1909, 14/10/72 Bundesgesetzblatt :

	Verordnung, 17/12/74	Bundesgesetzblatt p.3591, 20/12/74
	Unfallverhütungsvorschrift (VBG1), 01/04/77	
	Unfallverhütungsvorschrift GUV 01, 01/04/79	
	Unfallverhütungsvorschrift UVV See 01/01/81 (UVV 1.1)	
	Röntgenverordnung, 08/01/87	Bundesgesetzblatt p.114, 14/01/87
	Gewerbeordnung	Bundesgesetzblatt p.426, 29/01/87
	Strahlenschutzverordnung 1989	Bundesgesetzblatt p.1322, 12/07/89
	Unfallverhütungsvorschrift VBG121, 01/01/90	
	Gesundheitsschutz-Bergverordnung,	Bundesgesetzblatt p.1751, 09/08/91
	Störfall-Verordnung consolidée, 20/09/91	Bundesgesetzblatt p.1891, 28/09/91
	Gentechnik-Sicherheitsverordnung, 24/10/90	Bundesgesetzblatt p.2340, 03/11/90
	Gefahrgutverordnung See, 24/07/91	Bundesgesetzblatt p.1714, 31/07/91
	Verordnung, 10/06/92	Bundesgesetzblatt p.1019, 17/06/92
	Gefahrstoffverordnung, 26/10/93	Bundesgesetzblatt p.1782, 30/10/93

DK	Lov N.292, 10/06/81 - om visse havneanlæg	
	Bekendgørelse N.646, 18/12/85 med senere ændringer	
	Bekendtgørelse N.711, 16/11/87 om sikkerhed mv. på havneanlæg	
	Arbejdstilsynets Bekendtgørelse N.746, 28/08/92 om brug af pers. værnemidler	
	Bekendtgørelse N.901, 11/11/92 om anvend. af pers. værnemidler på havneanlæg	
	Søfartsstyrelsens tekniske forskrift N.7, 15/12/92	
	Lov N.177, 14/04/93 - arbejdsmiljø	

E	Real Decreto 773/1997 Utilización por los trabajadores de equipos de protección 30/5/97	Boletín Oficial del Estado 12/6/97, p 18

EL	Décret Présidentiel N.149, 14/3/34	22/03/34
	Loi N. 1568/85, 11/10/85	Journal Officiel p.3335, 18/10/85
	Loi N. 1836/89, 14/03/89	Journal Officiel p.1071, 14/03/89
	Décret Présidentiel N.225/89, 25/04/89	Journal Officiel p.3277, 02/05/89
	Décret Présidentiel N.395/94, 17/12/94	Journal Officiel p.3977, 19/12/94

F	Loi N.91-1414 du 31/12/91	Journal Officiel du 07/01/92
	Loi N.91-1414, 31/12/91	Journal Officiel N.319/92
	Décret N.93-41, 11/01/93	Journal Officiel, 13/01/93

	Arrêté, 19/03/93	

FIN	Valtioneuvoston päätös henkilönsuojainten valinnasta ja käytöstä työssä 93/1407, 22/12/93	

I	Decreto Legislativo N.626, 19/09/94	Supplemento Ordinario alla Gazzetta Ufficiale p.3, N.141, 12/11/94

IRL	The Safety, Health and Welfare at Work (General Applications) Regulations, 1993	Statutory Instruments NO 44 of 1993

L	Règlement Grand Ducal 04/11/94	Mémorial A N.96, p.1830, 17/11/94

NL	Arbeidsomstandigheden besluit Persoonlijke Beschermingsmiddelen, 15/07/93	Staatsblad N.442

P	Decreto-lei N.348/93, 01/10/93	Diário da República I Serie A, N.231, p.5553, 01/10/93
	Portaria N.988/93, 06/10/93	Diário Da República I Serie B, N.234, p.5599, 06/10/93
	Decreto-lei N.348/93, 07/09/93	Diário da República p. 5553, 01/10/93
	Portaria N.988/93, 10/09/93	Diário Da República p. 5599, 06/10/93
	Decreto-lei N.348/93, 01/10/93	Diário da República N. 231, p.5553, 01/10/93
	Decreto-lei N.348/93, 07/09/93	Diário da República p.5553, 01/10/93
	Decreto-lei N.988/93, 10/09/93	Diário da República p.5599, 06/10/93
	Portaria N.988/93, 01/10/93	Diário Da República I Serie A,N. 231, p. 5599, 06/10/93

S	Arbetsmiljölag 1977:1160, 19/12/77 Arbetsmiljöförordning 1977:1166, 19/12/77 Kungörelse med almänna föreskrifter om anvåndning av personlig skyddsutrustning 28/10/93	AFS 1993:40, p.3, 14/12/93

UK	The Health and Safety at Work (N.I.) Order 1978 of 25/07/78	Statutory Instrument N.1039 of 1978
	The Control of Lead at Work Regu. 1980 of 18/08/80	Statutory Instrument N.1248 of 1980
	The Ionising Radiations Regu. (N.I.) 1985	Statutory Rules of N.I. N.273 of 1985
	The Ionising Radiations Regu. 1985 of 23/08/85	Statutory Instrument N.1333 of 1985
	The Control of Lead at Work Regu. (N.I.) 1986	Statutory Rules of N.I. N.36 of 1986
	The Control of Asbestos at Work Regu. 1987 of 03/12/87	Statutory Instrument N.2115 of 1987
	The Control of Asbestos at Work Regu. (N.I.) 1988	Statutory Rules of NI N.74 of 1988
	The Control of Substances Hazardous to Health Regulations 1988 of 26/09/88	Statutory Instrument N.1657 of 1988
	The Construction (Head Protection) Regu. 1989 of 27/11/89	Statutory Instrument N.2209 of 1989
	The Noise at Work Regulations 1989 of 02/10/89	Statutory Instrument N.1790 of 1989
	The Construction (Head Protection) Regu. (N.I.) 1990	Statutory Rules of N.I. N.424 of 1990
	The Noise at Work Regulations 1990	Statutory Rules of N.I. N.147 of 1990
	The Control of Substances Hazardous to Health Regulations (N.I.) 1990	Statutory Rules of N.I. N.374 of 1990
	The Management of Health and Safety at Work Regulations 1992	Statutory Instrument N.2051 of 1992
	The Workplace (Health, Safety and Welfare Regulations 1992	Statutory Instrument N.3004 of 1992
	The Provision and Use of Work Equipment Regulations 1992	Statutory Instrument N.2932 of 1992
	The Personal Protective Equipment at Work Regulations 1992	Statutory Instrument N.2966 of 1992
	The Management of Health and Safety at Work Regu. (N.I) 1992	Statutory Rules of N.I. N.459 of 1992
	The Personal Protective Equipment at Work Regu. (N.I.) 1993	Statutory Rules of NI N.20 of 1993
	The Health and Safety at Work Etc. Act 1994	

HEALTH AND SAFETY AT WORK - THE WORKPLACE AND CATEGORIES OF WORKERS PARTICULARLY AT RISK

Manual handling of loads involving risk

Council Directive 90/269/EEC of 29 May 1990 on the minimum health and safety requirements for the manual handling of loads where there is a risk particularly of back injury to workers (fourth individual Directive within the meaning of Article 16(1) of Directive 89/391/EEC).

1) Deadline for implementation of the legislation in the Member States

31.12.92

2) References

Official Journal L 156, 21.06.90

A	Bundesgesetz über Sicherheit und Gesundheitsschutz bei der Arbeit	Bundesgesetzblatt, S. 3785, 17/06/94

B	Arrêté Royal du/Koninklijk Besluit van 12/08/93, N.93-2268	Moniteur Belge du/Belgisch Staatsblad van 29/09/93

D	Unfallverhütungsvorschrift (VBG1), 01/04/77 Unfallverhütungsvorschrift GUV 01, 01/04/79 Unfallverhütungsvorschrift, (VBG 103), 01/10/82 Unfallverhütungsvorschrift, (GUV 8.1), 01/09/82 Gesundheitsschutz-Bergverordnung, 31/07/91 Unfallverhütungsvorschrift, (GUV 7.8), 01/01/93 Unfallverhütungsvorschrift, (VBG 126), 01/01/93	Bundesgesetzblatt p.1751, 09/08/91

DK	Lov N.292, 10/06/81 om visse havneanlæg Bekendtgørelse N.646, 18/12/85 med senere ændringer Bekendtgørelse N.711, 16/11/87 om sikkerhed mv. på havneanlæg Bekendtgørelse N.746, 28/08/92 om brug af personlige værnemidler Bekendtgørelse N.1164, 16/12/92 Bekendtgørelse N.1181, 18/12/92 om arbejdets udførelse Søfartsstyrelsens tekniske forskrift N.7, 15/12/92 Bekendtgørelse N.60, 12/02/93 om manuel håndtering af byrder på havneanlæg Lov N.177, 14/04/93 - arbejdsmiljø Forholdsregler for civil søfart, BL 5-44, 16/06/94	

E	Real Decreto 487/1997 sobre disposiciones mínimas de seguridad y de salud relativas a la manipulación manual de cargas que entrañe riesgos en particular dorso-lumbares, para los trabajadores, 14/4/97	Boletín Oficial del Estado 23/4/97, p 3

EL	Décret Présidentiel N.149, 14/3/34 Loi N. 1568/85, 11/10/85 Loi N. 1836/89, 14/03/89 Loi N. 1837/89, 23/03/89 Décision N.13062/90, 07/03/90 Décret Présidentiel N.397/94, 17/12/94	22/03/34 Journal Officiel p.3335, 18/10/85 Journal Officiel p.1071, 14/03/89 Journal Officiel p.1105, 23/03/89 Journal Officiel p.187, 08/03/90 Journal Officiel p.3985, 19/12/94

F	Décret N.92-958, 03/09/92 Arrêté, 29/01/93 Décret N.82-958, 03/09/82 Arrêté, 29/01/93	Journal Officiel, 13/02/93 Journal Officiel N.2729/93

FIN	Valtioneuvoston päästös käsin tehtävistä nostoiosta ja siirroista työssä 93/1409, 22/12/93 Työturvallisuuslaki 58/299, 22/06/58, muutos 93/144, 29/01/93 Työterveyshuomtolaki 78/743, 29/09/78	

I	Decreto Legislativo N.626, 19/09/94	Supplemento Ordinario alla Gazzetta Ufficiale N.141, p.3, 12/11/94

IRL	The Safety, Health and Welfare at Work (General Application) Regulations, 1993	Statutory Instrument N.44 of 1993

L	Règlement Grand Ducal 04/11/94	Mémorial A N.96, p.1850, 17/11/94

NL	Besluit N.68, 27/01/93 Besluit N. DGA/AIB/WJZ/G/16648	Staatsblad 68/93

P	Decreto-lei N.330/93, 25/09/93	Diário da República I Serie A. N.226, p.5391, 25/09/93

S	Arbetsmiljölag 1977:1160, 19/12/77 Arbetsmiljöförordning 1977:1166, 19/12/77 Kungörelse om arbetsställningnar och arbetsörelser, 25/03/83 Kungörelse om arbetsställningnar och arbetsörelser, 25/11/93	AFS 1983:6, p.3, 11/05/83 AFS 1993:38, p.3, 17/12/93

UK	The Health and Safety at Work etc. Act. 1974	
	The Safety Representatives and Safety Committees Regu. 1977 of 16/03/77	Statutory Instrument N.500 of 1977
	The Health and Safety at Work (N.I.) Order 1978 of 25/07/78	Statutory Instrument N.1039 of 1978
	The Safety Representatives and Safety Committees Regulations 1979, 12/12/79	Statutory Rules of N.I. N.437 of 1979
	The Management of Health and Safety at Wirl Regu. 1992	Statutory Instrument N.2051 of 1992
	The Workplace (Health, Safety and Welfare) Regu. 1992	Statutory Instrument N.3004 of 1992
	The Provision and use of Work Equipment Regulations 1992	Statutory Instrument N.2932 of 1992
	The Manuel Handling Operations Regulations 1992 of 05/11/92	Statutory Instrument N.2793 of 1992
	The manual Handling Operations Regu. (N.I.) 1992 of 10/12/92	Statutory Rules of N.I. N.535 of 1992
	The Management of Health and Safety at Work Regu. (N.I.) 1992 of 26/10/92	Statutory Rules of N.I. N.459 of 1992

HEALTH AND SAFETY AT WORK - THE WORKPLACE AND CATEGORIES OF WORKERS PARTICULARLY AT RISK

Work with display screen equipment

Council Directive 90/270/EEC of 29 May 1990 on the minimum safety and health requirements for work with display screen equipment (fifth individual Directive within the meaning of Article 16(1) of Directive 89/391/EEC).

1) Deadline for implementation of the legislation in the Member States

31.12.92

2) References

Official Journal L 156, 21.06.90

A	Bundesgesetz über Sicherheit und Gesundheitsschutz bei der Arbeit	Bundesgesetzblatt, S. 3785, 17/06/94

B	Arrêté Royal du/Koninklijk Besluit van 27/08/93, N.2082/93	Moniteur Belge du/Belgisch Staatsblad van 07/09/93, N.50

D	Unfallverhütungsvorschrift (VBG1), 01/04/77 Unfallverhütungsvorschrift GUV 01, 01/04/79 Gesundheitsschutz-Bergverordnung, Sicherheitsregeln (ZH 1/618)	Bundesgesetzblatt p.1751, 09/08/91, 10/80

DK	Lov N.292, 10/06/81 om visse havneanlæg Bekendtgørelse N.646, 18/12/85 med senere ændringer Bekendtgørelse N.77, 16/11/87 om sikkerhed mv. på havneanlæg Bekendtgørelse N.1108, 15/12/92 om arbejde ved skærmterminaler Bekendtgørelse N.1163, 16/12/92 om faste arbejdssteders indretning Bekendtgørelse N.1165, 16/12/92 om arbejdsmedicinske undersøgelser Bekendtgørelse N.1181, 18/12/92 om arbejdets udførelse Bekendtgørelse N.1182, 18/12/92 om virksomhedernes sikkerheds- og sundhedsarbejde Bekendtgørelse N.58, 09/02/93 om arbejde ved skærmterminaler på havneanlæg Lov N.177, 14/04/93 - arbejdsmiljø	
E	Real Decreto 488/1997, sobre disposiciones mínimas de seguridad y salud relativas al trabajo con aquipos que incluyen pantallas de visualisación 14/4/97	Boletín Oficial del Estado 23/4/97, p 4
EL	Loi N. 1568/85, 11/10/85 Loi N. 1836/89, 14/03/89 Loi N. 1767/89, 04/04/88 Décision N.130558/89, 12/06/89 Décret Présidentiel N.398/94, 17/12/94	Journal Officiel p.3335, 18/10/85 Journal Officiel p.1071, 14/03/89 Journal Officiel p.709, 06/04/88 Journal Officiel Journal Officiel p.3987, 19/12/94
F	Décret N.91-451, 14/05/91 Circulaire DRT N°91/18, 4/11/91	Journal Officiel, 16/05/91 p 6497

FIN	Työturvallisuuslaki 58/299, muutos 93/144 Työterveyshuoltolaki 78/743, 29/09/78 Valtioneuvoston päästös työnantajan velvollisuudeksi säädetystä työterveyshuollosta 78/1009, 14/12/78 Valtioneuvoston päästös terveystarkastuksista erittyistä sairastumisen vaaraa aiheuttavissa töissä 92/1672 30/12/92 Laki työsuojelun valvonnasta ja muutoksenhausta työsuojeluasioissa 73/131, uusi nimi 87/29 Valtioneuvoston päästös näyttöpäätetyöstä 93/1405, 22/12/93	

I	Decreto Legislativo N.626, 19/09/94	Supplemento Ordinario alla Gazzetta Ufficiale N.141, p.3, 12/11/94

IRL	The Safety, Health and Welfare at Work (General Application) Regulations, 1993	Statutory Instrument N.44 of 1993

L	Règlement Grand Ducal 04/11/94	Mémorial A N.96, p.1853, 17/11/94

NL	Besluit N. 677, 01/01/93 Besluit N. DGA/AIB/WJZ/92/10579	Staatsblad 677/92

P	Decreto-lei N.349/93, 01/10/93	Diário da República I Serie A, p.5554, 01/10/93
	Portaria N.989/93, 06/10/93	Diário da República I Serie B, p.4603, 06/10/93
	Decreto-lei N.349/93, 07/09/93	Diário da República p. 5554, 01/10/93
	Portaria N.989/93, 10/09/93	Diário da República p.5603, 06/10/93
	Decreto-lei N.349/93, 01/10/93	Diário da República N. 231, p.5604, 01/10/93
	Portaria N.988/93, 06/10/93	Diário Da República I Serie B,N. 234, p. 5603, 6/10/93
	Decreto-lei N.989/93, 10/09/93	Diário da República p.5603, 06/10/93

S	Arbetsmiljölag,	Svensk författningfssamling (SFS) 1977:1160
	Arbetsmiljöförordning	Svensk författningfssamling (SFS) 1977:1966
	Arbetarskyddsstyrelsens kungörelse med	Arbetarskyddsstyrelsens författningfssamling
	föreskrifter om interkontroll av arbetsmiljön	(AFS) 1992:6
	Arbetarskyddsstyrelsens kungörelse med	Arbetarskyddsstyrelsens författningfssamling
	föreskrifter om arbete vid bildskärm	(AFS) 1992:14

UK	The Health and Safety at Work etc. Act. 1974	
	The Safety Representatives and Safety Committees Regu. 1977 of 16/03/77	Statutory Instrument N.500 of 1977
	The Safety Representatives and Safety Committees Regulations 1979, 12/12/79	Statutory Rules of N.I. N.437 of 1979
	The Management of Health and Safety at Work Regu. (N.I.) 1992 of 26/10/92	Statutory Rules of N.I. N.459 of 1992
	The Health and Safety (Display Screen Equipment) 1992	Statutory Instrument N.2792 of 1992
	The National Health Service (General Ophthalmic Services) Regualtions 1986	Statutory Instrument N.975 of 1986
	The National Health Service Amendment 1989	Statutory Instrument N.1175 of 1989
	The General Ophtmalmic Services Regulations 1986, N.163	Statutory Rules of Northern Ireland 1986

PROTECTION OF HEALTH AND SAFETY AT WORK - DANGEROUS AGENTS

Exposure to carcinogens

Council Directive 90/394/EEC of 28 June 1990 on the protection of workers from the risks related to exposure to carcinogens at work (sixth individual Directive within the meaning of Article 16(1) of Directive 89/391/EEC).

Council Directive 97/42/EC of 27 June 1997 amending for the first time Directive 90/394/EEC on the protection of workers from the risks related to exposure to carcinogens at work (Sixth individual Directive within the meaning of Article 16 (1) of Directive 89/391/EEC).

1) Deadline for implementation of the legislation in the Member States

Directive 90/394/EEC: 31.12.1992

Directive 97/42/EC: 27.06.2000

2) References

Official Journal L 196, 26.07.1990

Official Journal L 179, 08.07.1997

A	Bundesgesetz über Sicherheit und Gesundheitsschutz bei der Arbeit	Bundesgesetzblatt, S. 3785, 17/06/94

B	Arrêté Royal du/Koninklijk Besluit van 02/12/93	Moniteur Belge du/Belgisch Staatsblad van 29/12/93, N.93-3006

D	Gefahrstoffverordnung vom 26/10/93	Bundesgesetzblatt (Teile I, II, III) Teil I N.57, 30/10/93

DK	Arbejdsministeriet bekendtgørelse N 1163 16/12/92 om faste arbejdssteders indretning Arbejdsministeriet bekendtgørelse N.1109 15/12/92 om anvendelse af tekniske hjoelpemilder Arbejdsministeriet bekendtgørelse N 693 14/10/91 om byggepladsers og lignende arbejdssteders indretning Arbejdsministeriet bekendtgørelse N 1181 af 18/12/92 om virksomhedernes sikkerheds og sundhedsarbejde Arbejdsministeriet bekendtgørelse N 1165 af 16/12/92 om arbejdsmedicinske undersøgelser efter lov om arbejdsmiljø Arbejdsministeriet bekendtgørelse N 646 18/12/85 Lov N 220 af 22/4/87 Lov N 380 af 13/6/90 Lov N 273 af 8/5/91 Lov 373 af 20/5/92 Lov N 474 af 24/6/92 Lov N 177 af 14/4/93 Arbejdsministeriet bekendtgørelse N 540 af 2/10/82 om stoffer og materialer Arbejdsministeriet bekendtgørelse N 1182 af 18/12/92 om arbejdets udførelse Bekendtgørelse N 300 af 12/5/93 om foranstaltninger til forebyggelse af kroeftrisikoen ved arbejde med stoffer og materialer mv	

E	Real Decreto N° 665/97 de 12/5/97 sobre la protección de los trabajadores contra les riesgos relacionados con la exposición a agentes cancerígenos durante el trabajo	Boletín Oficial del Estado N° 124, 24/5/97, p.16111

EL	Décret présidentiel N.61/75 de 1975 Décret présidentiel N.1179/80 de 1980 Décret présidentiel N.329/83 de 1983 Loi N.1568/85 de 1985 Décret présidentiel N.70A/88 de 1988 Loi N.1836/1989, 14/03/89 Décision ministérielle N.1197/89 de 1989 Décret présidentiel N 399/94	FEK N 221/A 17/12/94 p 3992-3996

F	Arrêté ministériel, 05/01/93	Journal Officiel, 19/02/93, p.2729

FIN	Valtioneuvoston päästös työhön liittyvän syöpävaaran torjunnasta 92/1182, 26/11/92 Työministeriön päästös syöpäsairauden vaaraa aiheuttavista tekijöistä 93/838, 16/09/93	Suomen Säädöskokoelma 7/12/92 Suomen Säädöskokoelma 30/9/93

I	Decreto Legislativo N.626, 19/09/94	Supplemento Ordinario alla Gazzetta Ufficiale N.141, 12/11/94

IRL	Safety, Health and Welfare at Work (Carcinogens) Regu. of 1993 European Communities (Protection of Workers) (Exposure to Asbestos) (Amendment) Regulations of 1993	Statutory Instrument N.80 of 1993 Statutory Instrument N.276 of 1993

L	Règlement Grand Ducal 04/11/94	Mémorial A N.96, p.1856, 17/11/94

NL	Besluit van 04/02/94 tot vaststelling van voorschriften terbescherming van werk nemers tegen de gevaren van te lootstelling aan krankerverwekkende stoffen en processen op het werk (Besluit kranverwekken de stoffen en processen)	Staatsblad 1994, 91

P	Decreto-lei N.390, 20/11/93	Diário da República I Aviso N.272, p.6462-6465, 20/11/93

S	Arbetsmiljölag, Arbetsmiljöförordning	Svensk författningfssamling (SFS) 1977:1160 Svensk författningfssamling (SFS) 1977:1166 Arbetarskyddsstyrelsens författningfssamling (AFS) 1980:11 ändring AFS 1993:7 Arbetarskyddsstyrelsens författningfssamling (AFS) 1980:12 Arbetarskyddsstyrelsens författningfssamling (AFS) 1981:12 Arbetarskyddsstyrelsens författningfssamling (AFS) 1983:10 Arbetarskyddsstyrelsens författningfssamling (AFS) 1984:8 Arbetarskyddsstyrelsens författningfssamling (AFS) 1985:1, 4, 17 Arbetarskyddsstyrelsens författningfssamling (AFS) 1988:7 Arbetarskyddsstyrelsens författningfssamling (AFS) 1990:13, 14 Arbetarskyddsstyrelsens författningfssamling (AFS) 1992:2 Arbetarskyddsstyrelsens författningfssamling (AFS) 1993:4, 9, 37

UK	The Control of Substances Hazardous to Health (Amendment) Regulations 1992 The Control of Substances Hazardous to Health (Amendment) Regulations 1993	Statutory Instrument 1992 N.I. N.2382, Health and Safety of 14/10/92 Statutory Instrument N.I N.41, Health and Safety of 05/02/93

HEALTH AND SAFETY AT WORK - DANGEROUS AGENTS

Exposure to biological agents

Council Directive 90/679/EEC of 26 November 1990 on the protection of workers from risks related to exposure to biological agents at work (7th individual Directive within the meaning of Article 16(1) of Directive 89/391/EEC).

Council Directive 93/88/EEC of 12 October 1993 amending Council Directive 90/679/EEC on the protection of workers from risks related to exposure to biological agents at work (7th individual Directive within the meaning of Article 16(1) of Directive 89/391/EEC).

Council Directive 95/30/EEC of 30 June 1995 amending Council Directive 90/679/EEC on the protection of workers from risks related to exposure to biological agents at work (7th individual Directive within the meaning of Article 16(1) of Directive 89/391/EEC).

Commission Directive 97/59/EC of 7 October 1997 adapting to technical progress Council Directive 90/679/EEC on the protection of workers from risks related to exposure to biological agents at work (seventh individual Directive within the meaning of Article 16 (1) of Directive 89/391/EEC).

Commission Directive 97/65/EC of 26 November 1997 adapting to technical progress Council Directive 90/679/EEC on the protection of workers from risks related to exposure to biological agents at work (seventh individual Directive within the meaning of Article 16 (1) of Directive 89/391/EEC).

1) Deadline for implementation of the legislation in the Member States

- Directive 90/679/EEC:
  28.11.1993
  28.11.1995: Portugal
- Directive 93/88/EEC:
  30.04.1994
  31.12.1995: Portugal
- Directive 95/30/EEC: 30.11.1996
- Directive 97/59/EC: 31.03.1998
- Directive 97/65/EC: 30.06.1998

2) References

Official Journal L 374, 31.12.1990
Official Journal L 268, 29.10.1993
Official Journal L 155, 06.07.1995

Official Journal L 282, 15.10.1997
Official Journal L 335, 06.12.1997

A	Bundesgesetz über Sicherheit und Gesundheitsschutz bei der Arbeit	Bundesgesetzblatt, S. 3785, 17/06/94

B	Arrêté Royal du 04/08/96	Moniteur belge du 01/10/96 p.25285

D	Verordnung zur Änderung der Verordnung über Immissionswerte, 27/5/94	

DK	Bekendtgørelse N.236, 02/05/73 Bekendtgørelse N.540, 02/09/82 Bekendtgørelse N.646, 18/12/85 Bekendtgørelse N.693, 14/10/91 Bekendtgørelse N.746, 28/08/92 Bekendtgørelse N.1126, 15/12/92 Bekendtgørelse N.1163, 16/12/92 Bekendtgørelse N.1165, 16/12/92 Bekendtgørelse N.775, 17/12/92 Bekendtgørelse N.1181, 18/12/92 Bekendtgørelse N.1182, 18/12/92 Bekendtgørelse N.290, 05/05/93 Bekendtgørelse N.864, 10/11/93	

E	Real Decreto 664/97 del 12/5/97	Boletín oficial del Estado N 124, 24/5/97 p 16100-16111

EL	Loi N.1568/85 du 1985 Décret présidentiel N.77/93 Décret présidentiel du 15/7/97	FEK A N 34 18/3/93 Journal officiel du 15/8/97 p.6279

F	Décret N.94-352 du 4/05/95 Arrêté du 18/07/94 Arrêté du 17/4/97 modifiant l'arrêté du 18/7/94 fixant la liste des agents biologiques pathogènes	Journal officiel, 06/05/94, p.6620 ff. Journal officiel, 30/07/94,p.11078 ff. Journal officiel, 26/4/97, p.6361

FIN	Valtioneuvoston päästös työntekijöiden suojelemisesta työhön liittyvältä biologisten tekijöiden aiheuttamalta vaaralta 93/1155, 9/12/93	Suomen Säädöskokoelma

I	Decreto Legislativo N.626, 19/09/94	Supplemento Ordinario alla Gazzetta Ufficiale N.141, 12/11/94

IRL	Safety, Health and Welfare at Work Regulations of 1994	Statutory Instrument N.146 of 1994

L	Règlement Grand Ducal 04/11/94	Mémorial A N.96, p.1816, 17/11/94

NL	Besluit Biologische Agentia van 17/05/94	Staatsblad N.368 van 1994

P	Decreto-Lei N.84/97 16/4/97	Diário da República I Série A N.89, 16/4/97 p.1702

S	Arbetsmiljölag, Arbetsmiljöförordning Biologiska Amnen, 1/9/92	Svensk författningfssamling (SFS) 1977:1160 Svensk författningfssamling (SFS) 1977:1166 Arbetarskyddsstyrelsens författningfssamling (AFS) 1992:8, ändring AFS 1993:18 AFS 1992:8, 1/9/92 p.1

UK	The Control of Substances Hazardous to Health Regulations 1994 Control of Substances Hazardous to Health Regulations (Nothern Ireland), 1995	Statutory Instruments 1994 Statutory Rules of Nothern Ireland 1995, N.51

EMPLOYMENT AND PAY - ATYPICAL WORK

Temporary workers: Health and safety

Council Directive 91/383/EEC of 25 June 1991 supplementing the measures to encourage improvements in the safety and health at work of workers with a fixed–duration employment relationship or a temporary employment relationship.

1) Deadline for implementation of the legislation in the Member States

31.12.92

2) References

Official Journal L 206, 29.08.91

A	Landarbeitsordnung Bundesgesetz über Sicherheit und Gesundheit bei der Arbeit (Arbeitnehmerinnenschutzgesetz-ASchG) Bediensteten-Schutzgesetz Landarbeitsordnung	Landesgesetzblatt für Niederösterreich N.9020-15 Bundesgesetzblatt N.450//94, 17/06/94 Landesgesetzblatt für Niederösterreich N.2015-1 Landesgesetzblatt für Niederösterreich N.9020-15
B	Loi du/Wet van 24/07/87 sur le travail temporaire, le travail intérimaire et la mise de travailleurs à la disposition d'utilisateurs Loi du/Wet van 30/03/94	Moniteur belge du/Belgisch Staatsblad van 24/07/87, p.982 Moniteur belge du/Belgisch Staatsblad van 31/03/94
D	Gesetz zur Umsetzung der EG- Rahmenrichtlinie Arbeitsschutz und weiterer Arbeitsschutz-Richtlinien, 07/08/96	Bundesgesetzblatt 20/08/1996, p.1248

DK	Lov om Arbejdsmiljø, Bekendtgørelse, 18/12/85 Søfartsstyrelsens tekniske forskrift N.7, 15/12/92 Bekendtgørelse, 18/12/92 om arbejdets udførelse Bekendtgørelse, 18/12/92 om virksomhedernes sikkerhed og sundhedsarbejde	
E	Orden, 09/03/71 Ley N.8, 10/03/80 Ley N.8 10/03/80 Ley 14/1994, por la que se regulan las empresas de trabajo temporal Ley N.31/1995, 08/11/95	Boletín Oficial del Estado, 16/03/71 Boletín Oficial del Estado, 14/03/80 Boletín Oficial del Estado, 14/03/80 Boletín Oficial del Estado N.269, 10/11/95
EL	Décret présidentiel N.17/96 du 18/01/96	Journal Officiel, N.11, Volume A, p.93, 18/01/96
F	Loi No. 90-316 du 20/07/90 favorisant la stabilité del'emploi par l'adaption du régime des contrats précaires Arrêté du 08/10/90 fixant la liste des travaux pour lesquels il ne peut faire appel aux salariés des entreprises de travail temporaire Code du travail, modifié par la Loi du 23/03/90 Arrêté du 11/07/77, "fixant la liste des traveaux nécessitant une surveillance médicale spéciale" Arrêté du 08/10/90 fixant la liste des travaux pour lesquels il ne peut être fait appel aux salariés sous contract de travail à durée determinée ou aux salariés des entreprises de travail temporaire Arrêté du 27/06/91 fixant la liste des travaux pour lesquels il ne peut être fait appel aux salariés sous contract de travail à durée determinée ou aux salariés des entreprises de travail temporaire	Journal Officiel du 08/11/90 Journal Officiel du 24/07/77 Journal Officiel du 09/11/90 Journal Officiel du 17/07/91

FIN	Työturvallisuuslaki 299/58, 28/06/58, muutokset 93/144 ja 93/509 Työsopimuslaki 320/70, 30/04/70 Työterveyshuoltolaki 743/78, 29/09/78	
I	Decreto legislativo N.626, 19/09/94 Decreto legislativo N.242, 19/03/96	Supplemento ordinario N.75 alla Gazetta Ufficiale, Serie generale del 06/05/96, N.104, p.3
IRL	The Safety, Health and Welfare at Work (General Application) Regulations 1993	Statutory Rules of Northern Ireland N.44, 1993
L	Loi, 17/06/94	Mémorial A N.55, 01/07/94
NL	Arbeidsomstandighedenwet Besluit Arbodiensten van 28/12/93 Besluit Bedrijfshulpverlening Arbeidsomstandighedenwet, 28/12/93 Ministeriele Regeling Certificatie Arbodiensten van 28/12/93 Ministeriele Regeling deskundigheidseisem van 28/12/93	Staatsblad N.757 Staatsblad N.782 Staatsblad N.783 Staatscourant N.252, 30/12/93, p.38 Staatscourant N.252, 30/12/93 p.38
P	Decreto-lei N.475/11-12, 25/01/67 Decreto-lei N.441/91, 14/11/91 Decreto-lei N.47511, 25/01/67 Decreto-lei N.47512, 25/01/67	Diário da República N.21, p.125-126, 02/02/67 Diário da República I A, N.262, p.5826, 14/11/91 Diário da República N.21, 00/01/67, p.125 Diário da República N.21, 00/01/67, p.126
S	Work Environment Act of 19/12/77, amended by Lag 1991:677	SFS 1977:1160

UK	Health and Safety at Work Act 1974	
	Health and Safety at Work (N.I.) Order of 25/7/78	Statutory Rules of Northern Ireland N.1039, 1978
	The Management of Health and Safety at Work Regulations, 26/08/92	Statutory Rules of Norhern Ireland N.2051, 1992
	Management of Health and Safety at Work Regulations of 26/10/92	Statutory Rules of Northern Ireland N.459 of 1992
	The Manual Handling Operations Regulations 1992 of 05/11/92	Statutory Rules of Northern Ireland N.2793, 1992
	The Provision and Use of Work Equipment Regulations 1992 of 17/11/92	Statutory Rules of Northern Ireland N.2932, 1992
	The Personal Protective Equipments at Work, Regulations of 25/11/92	Statutory Rules of Northern Ireland N.2966, 1992
	The Workplace (Health, Safety and Welfare) Regulations 1992 of 01/12/92	Statutory Rules of Northern Ireland N.3004, 1992
	Management of Health and Safety at Work Regulations of 26/08/92	Statutory Instruments N.2051, 1992
	The Workplace (Health, Safety and Welfare) Regulations 1992 of 01/12/92	Statutory Instruments N.3004, 1992
	The Provision and Use of Work Equipment Regulations 1992 of 17/11/92	Statutory Instruments N.2932, 1992
	The Personal Protective Equipment of Work Regulations of 25/11/92	Statutory Instruments N.2966, 1992
	The Manual Handling Operations Regulations 1992 of 05/11/92	Statutory Instruments N.2793, 1992
	Management of Health and Safety at Work Regulations, Legal notice number 11 of 1996	Gibraltar Gazette N.2894, 25/01/96

HEALTH AND SAFETY AT WORK - THE WORKPLACE AND CATEGORIES OF WORKERS PARTICULARLY AT RISK

Improved medical assistance on board vessels

Council Directive 92/29/EEC of 31 March 1992 on the minimum health and safety requirements for improved medical treatment on board vessels.

1) Deadline for implementation of the legislation in the Member States

31.12.1994

2) References

Official Journal L 113, 30.04.1992

A	Bundesgesetz vom 19/3/81 über die Seeschiffart und über eine Änderung des Handelsgesetzbuches, des Verkehrs-Arbeitsinspektionsgesetze und des Bundesgesetzes zur Erfüllung des Internationales Übereinkommens von 1960 zum Schutz des menschlichen Lebens auf See, der Regeln zur Verhütung von Zusammenstössen auf See sowie des Internationalen Freibord-übereinkommens von 1966	Bundesgesetzblatt für die Republik Österreich Nr.174/81, 7/4/81
	Verordnung des Bundesministers für Verkehr vom 8/4/81 über die Seeschiffart	Bundesgesetzblatt für die Republik Österreich Nr.189/81, 13/4/81
B		
D	Gesetz, 09/08/94	Bundesgesetsblatt Teil I N.54, S.2071, 16/08/94

DK	Bekendtgørelse Nr.528 AF 26/6/95	

E	Reglemento Organica de Sanidad Exterior 7/9/34	Gacetas 16, 17, 18 y 19/09/34
	Orden 28/10/46	Boletín Oficial del Estado N.317, 13/11/46
	Orden 20/05/69	Boletín Oficial del Estado N.160, 05/07/69
	Orden 19/12/74	Boletín Oficial del Estado N.305, 21/12/74
	Convenio Internacional 01/11/74	Boletín Oficial del Estado N.144, 16/06/80
	Convenio n° 164 de la Conferencia Internacional del trabajo	Boletín Oficial del Estado N.18, 21/01/91, p.2050
	Real Decreto N.1414/1981, 03/07/81 (1660)	Boletín Oficial del Estado N.169, 16/7/81 p. 1659
	Orden de la Presidencia de Gobierno 04/12/80	Boletín Oficial del Estado N.22, 26/01/81
	Orden que modifica la orden 4/12/80, 17/07/82	Boletín Oficial del Estado N.172, 20/07/82
	Orden Ley Autonomica Presidencia del Gobierno 17/07/82	
	Orden 10/06/83	
	Orden 09/03/71	Boletín Oficial del Estado N.16, 17-4-7
	Orden 16/01/61	Boletín Oficial del Estado N.237, 28/01/61
	Orden 26/07/63	
	Real Decreto N.917/92, 17/07/92 (20364)	Boletín Oficial del Estado N.206, 27/08/92
	Real Decreto N.918/92, 17/07/92 (20365)	Boletín Oficial del Estado N.206, 27/08/92 p. 29811
	Real Decreto N.919/92, 17/07/92 (20366)	Boletín Oficial del Estado N.206, 27/08/92
	Real Decreto N.924/92, 17/07/92 (20371)	Boletín Oficial del Estado N.206, 27/08/92
	Orden 08/04/76	
	Orden 31/07/76	Boletín Oficial del Estado, 22/04/76
	Orden 09/10/78	
	Real Decreto N.925/92, 17/07/92	Boletín Oficial del Estado, 14/11/78
	Real Decreto N.926/92, 17/07/92, (20373)	Boletín Oficial del Estado N.206, 27/08/92

EL	Décret présidentiel N 376/95, 11/9/95	FEK A N 206, 5/10/95 p.6167

F	Loi 83.581 du 5/7/83 sur la sauvegarde de la vie humaine en mer, l'habitabilité à bord des navires et la prévention de la pollution Règlement annexé à l'arrêté du 23/11/87 relatif à la sécurité des navires Code du travail maritime, articles 2 et 3 p 1813 Arrêté du 9/7/92 Loi 93.121 du 27/1/1993 (DMOS) Décret N 67-690 du 7/4/67 relatif aux conditions d'exercice de la profession de marin	
FIN	Työturvallisuuslaki 58/299, muutos 93/509 Asetus aluksen miehityksestä ja laivahenkilökunnan pätevyydestä 84/250, 16/3/84 Merenkulkuhallituksen päätös laiva-apteekista 1743/80/317, 20/9/85	
I	Decreto interministeriale del 25/5/88	Gazzetta Ufficiale - serie generale 21/7/88 N.70
IRL		
L		
NL	Besluit van 1/9/95 Besluit van 13/11/95 Regeling medische uitrusting aan boord vanvisersvaartuigen	Staatsblad Nr.465 van 95 Staatsblad Nr.557 van 95 Staatsblad Nr.233 van 30/11/95

P	Decreto-lei N. 274/95 de 23/10/95 Portaria numero 006/97 de 2/1/97	Diário da República I Aviso N.245 de 23/10/95 Diário da República I Série B

S	Sjöfartsverkets kungörelse med föreskrifter och allmänna råd om sjukvård och apotek på fartyg Sjöfartsverkets kungörelse med föreskrifter och allmänna råd om besättningens bostäder på fartyg m.m., Sjöfartsverkets kungörelse med föreskrifter och allmänna råd om transport till sjöss av farligt gods i förpackad form m.m.	Sjöfartsverkets författningssamling (SJÖFS) 1994:6 Sjöfartsverkets författningssamling (SJÖFS) 1992:6 Sjöfartsverkets författningssamling (SJÖFS) 1990:23, ändring SJÖFS 1992:14, 1994:1, 1995:2

UK	The Merchant Shipping and Fishing Vessels (Medicalstores) Regulation of 14/7/95	S.I. NO 1802 of 1995

HEALTH AND SAFETY AT WORK - THE WORKPLACE AND CATEGORIES OF WORKERS PARTICULARLY AT RISK

Temporary and mobile work sites

Council Directive 92/57/EEC of 24 June 1992 on the implementation of minimum safety and health requirements at temporary or mobile work sites (eighth individual Directive within the meaning of Article 16 of Directive 89/391/EEC).

1) Deadline for implementation of the legislation in the Member States

31.12.93

2) References

Official Journal L 245, 26.08.92

A	Verordnung über den Nachweis der Fachkenntnisse für bestimmte Arbeiten	Bundesgesetzblatt, 06/06/75
	Kesselgesetz	Bundesgesetzblatt S.1041, 24/04/92
	Bauarbeiterschutzverordnung	Bundesgesetzblatt S.3355, 05/05/94
	Arbeitnehmerinnenschutzgesetz	Bundesgesetzblatt S.3785, 17/06/94
	Bundesgesetz 434 zur Änderung des Mutterschutzgesetzes und das Eltern Karenzurlaubsgesetz	Bundesgesetzblatt S.6263, 30/06/95
	Allgemeine Arbeitnehmerschutzverordnung	Bundesgesetzblatt, 11/03/83
	Druckluft und Taucherarbeiten-Verordnung	Bundesgesetzblatt S.2535, 11/10/73
	Elektroschutzverordnung 1995-ESV 1995	Bundesgesetzblatt S 237 p.8381, 25/10/95
	Betrieb von Starkstromanlagen - grundsätzliche Bestimmungen	Österreichische Bestimmungen fûr die Elektrotechnik ÖVE-E-5, Teil 1/1989, N 47 p.696 20/1/94
	Sonderbestimmungen für den Betrieb elektrischer Anlagen in explosionsgefährdeten Betriebstätten	Österreichische Bestimmungen fûr die Elektrotechnik ÖVE-E-5, Teil 9/1982, N 47 p.721 20/1/94
	Betrieb elektrischer Bahnanlagen	Österreichische Bestimmungen fûr die Elektrotechnik ÖVE-T 5/1990, p.1770, 20/1/94
	Errichtung von Starkstromanlagen mit Nennpannungen bis 1000 V und 1500 V	Österreichische Bestimmungen fûr die Elektrotechnik ÖVE-EN 1, Teil 1/1989, p.913 20/1/94

	Nachtrag A zu den Bestimmungen über Errichtung von Starkstromanlagen bis 1000 V und 1500 V	Österreichische Bestimmungen für die Elektrotechnik ÖVE-EN 1, Teil 3/1986, p.1031 20/1/94
	Nachtrag A und Nachtrag B zu den Bestimmungen über Errichtung von Starkstromanlagen mit Nennspannungen bis 1000 V und 1500 V	Österreichische Bestimmungen für die Elektrotechnik ÖVE-EN 1, Teil 3/1985, p.1052 20/1/94
	Errichtung von Starkstromanlagen mit Nennpannungen bis 1000 V und 1500 V Teil 4: Anlagen besonderer Art	Österreichische Bestimmungen für die Elektrotechnik ÖVE-EN 1, Teil 4/1980, p.1063 20/1/94
	Errichtung von Starkstromanlagen mit Nennpannungen bis 1000 V und 1500 V Teil 4: besondere Anlagen	Österreichische Bestimmungen für die Elektrotechnik ÖVE-EN 1, Teil 4, p.1078, 20/1/94
	Errichtung von elektrischer Anlagen in explosionsgefährdeten Bereichen	Österreichische Bestimmungen für die Elektrotechnik ÖVE-EX 65/1981, p.1276, 20/1/94
	Nachtrag A zu den Bestimmungen über die Errichtung elektrischer Anlagen in explosionsgefährdeten Bereichen	Österreichische Bestimmungen für die Elektrotechnik ÖVE-EX 65a/1985, p.1303, 20/1/94
	Errichtung von Starkstromanlagen mit Nennspannung über 1 kV	Österreichische Bestimmungen für die Elektrotechnik ÖVE-EH 1/1982, p.823, 20/1/94
	Nachtrag A zu den Bestimmungen über die Errichtung von Starkstromanlagen mit Nennspannung über 1 kV	Österreichische Bestimmungen für die Elektrotechnik ÖVE-EH 1a/1987, p.861, 20/1/94

B	Loi relative au bien-être des travailleurs lors de l'exécution de leur travail 4/8/96	Moniteur belge 18/9/96

D	Musterbauordnung-MBO, Fassung Dezember 1993 Arbeitsstättenverordnung, 20/03/75 Unfallverhütungsvorschrift Rammen-VBG 41, 01/04/80	
		Sammlung der Einzel-Unfallverhütungs-vorschriften der gewerblichen Genossenschaften, p.1
	Unfallverhütungsvorschrift Steinbrüche, Gräbereien, VGB 42, 01/10/84	Sammlung der Einzel-Unfallverhütungsvors-chriften der gewerblichen Genossenschaften, p.1
	VBG 43, 01/04/84	Sammlung der Einzel-Unfallverhütungsvors-chriften der gewerblichen Genossenschaften, p.1
	VBG 1 - Allgemeine Vorschriften, 01/04/77	Sammlung der Einzel-Unfallverhütungsvors chriften der gewerblichen Genossenschaften, p.1
	VBG 4 - Elektrische Anlagen und Betreibsmittel, 01/04/79	Sammlung der Einzel-Unfallverhütungsvors chriften der gewerblichen Genossenschaften, p.1
	VBG 5 - Kraftbetriebene Arbeitsmittel, 01/10/85	Sammlung der Einzel-Unfallverhütungsvors chriften der gewerblichen Genossenschaften, p.1
	VBG 7, 01/04/77	Sammlung der Einzel-Unfallverhütungsvors chriften der gewerblichen Genossenschaften, p.1
	VBG 44 - Tragbare Eintreibgeräte, 01/04/84	Sammlung der Einzel-Unfallverhütungsvors chriften der gewerblichen Genossenschaften, p.1
	VBG 7 Nr. 6, 01/05/54	Sammlung der Einzel-Unfallverhütungsvors chriften der gewerblichen Genossenschaften, p.1
	VBG 45 - Arbeiten mit Schußapparaten, 01/04/90	Sammlung der Einzel-Unfallverhütungsvors chriften der gewerblichen Genossenschaften, p.1
	VBG 74, 01/10/92	Sammlung der Einzel-Unfallverhütungsvors chriften der gewerblichen Genossenschaften, p.1
	VBG 109 - Erste Hilfe, 01/10/94	Sammlung der Einzel-Unfallverhütungsvors chriften der gewerblichen Genossenschaften, p.1
	VBG 125, 01/04/95	Sammlung der Einzel-Unfallverhütungsvors chriften der gewerblichen Genossenschaften, p.1
	VBG 7tl, 01/05/63	Sammlung der Einzel-Unfallverhütungsvors chriften der gewerblichen Genossenschaften, p.1
	VBG 8, 01/04/80	Sammlung der Einzel-Unfallverhütungsvors chriften der gewerblichen Genossenschaften, p.1
	VBG 9, 01/12/74	Sammlung der Einzel-Unfallverhütungsvors chriften der gewerblichen Genossenschaften, p.1
	VBG 12, 01/10/90	Sammlung der Einzel-Unfallverhütungsvors chriften der gewerblichen Genossenschaften, p.1
	VBG 14, 01/04/77	Sammlung der Einzel-Unfallverhütungsvors chriften der gewerblichen Genossenschaften, p.1
	VBG 15, 01/04/90	Sammlung der Einzel-Unfallverhütungsvors chriften der gewerblichen Genossenschaften, p.1
	VBG 35, 01/04/83	Sammlung der Einzel-Unfallverhütungsvors chriften der gewerblichen Genossenschaften, p.1
	VBG 37, 01/04/77	Sammlung der Einzel-Unfallverhütungsvors chriften der gewerblichen Genossenschaften, p.1

	VBG 40, 01/04/76	Sammlung der Einzel-Unfallverhütungsvors chriften der gewerblichen Genossenschaften, p.1
	VBG 40a, 01/10/70	Sammlung der Einzel-Unfallverhütungsvors chriften der gewerblichen Genossenschaften, p.1
	Betriebsverfassungsgesetz 15060, 15/01/72	Bundesgesetzblatt I, p.13
	Schwerbehindertengesetz 15500, in der Fassung der Bekanntmachung vom 26/08/86	Bundesgesetzblatt I, p.1421
	Mutterschutzgesetz, in der Fassung der Bekanntmachung vom 18/04/68	Bundesgesetzblatt I, p.315
	Unfallverhütungsvorschrift, Sicherheits- und Gesundheits-schutzkennzeichnung - UVV 1.5, 21/06/96	
	Bergverordnung für alle bergbaulichen Betriebe (allg. Bundesverordnung - ABBergV), 23/10/95	Bundesgesetzblatt I, p.1466
	Zweite Verordnung zur Änderung der VO zum Schutz vor gefährlichen Stoffen, 19/09/94	
	Gesetzbeschluß des Deutschen Bundestages, 13/06/96	Bundesrat Drucksache 427/96, 14/06/96
	VBG 125 - Unfallverhütungsvorschrift, 01/04/95	UVV - Sicherheits- und Gesundheits-schutzkennzeichnung am Arbeitsplatz, p.1
	GUV 0.7 - Unfallverhütungsvorschrift, 00/09/94	Bundesverband der Unfallversicherungsträger der öffentlichen Hand - BAGUV 0.7, p.1

DK	Bekendtgørelse N.501, 05/10/78	Lovtidende, 05/10/78
	Bekendtgørelse N.694, 07/08/92	Lovtidende, 07/08/92
	Bekendtgørelse N.775, 17/09/92	Lovtidende, 17/09/92
	Bekendtgørelse N.1109, 15/12/92	Lovtidende, 15/12/92
	Bekendtgørelse N.1163, 16/12/92	Lovtidende, 16/12/92
	Bekendtgørelse N.1181-1182, 18/12/92	Lovtidende, 18/12/92
	Bekendtgørelse N.290, 05/05/93	Lovtidende, 05/05/93
	Bekendtgørelse N.1017, 15/12/93	Lovtidende, 15/12/93

E	Ordenanza de trabajo en la construcción, 31/01/40	Boletín Oficial del Estado,p.147, 03/02/40
	Ordenanza General de Seguridad e Higiene en el trabajo	
	Estatuto de los trabajadores	
	Ley 08/88, 07/04/88	
	Orden de 09/06/71	Boletín Oficial del Estado,p.1336
	Decreto de 11/03/71	Boletín Oficial del Estado,p.681
	Orden de 20/01/56	Boletín Oficial del Estado,p.243, 02/02/56
	Orden de 23/05/77	Boletín Oficial del Estado,p.1806, 14/06/77
	Real Decreto 555/86, 21/02/86	Boletín Oficial del Estado,p.2022, 21/03/86
	Real Decreto 84/90, 19/01/90	Boletín Oficial del Estado,p.2357, 25/01/90
	Orden de 15/02/84	Boletín Oficial del Estado,p.1093

	Ley 13/82, 07/04/82 Ordenanza de Trabajo de la construcción Vidrio y Cerámica, 28/08/70 Instrumento de ratificación del Convenio N.62 de la OIT, 12/06/59	Boletín Oficial del Estado,p.1677, 09/09/70 Boletín Oficial del Estado,p.1141, 20/02/59
EL	Décret Présidentiel N.778/80, 19/08/80 Décret Présidentiel N.1073/81, 12/09/81 Loi N.1396, 13/09/83 Loi N.1568/85, 11/10/85 Décret Présidentiel N.225/89, 25/04/89 Décret Présidentiel N.305, 29/08/96	Journal Officiel p.2377, 26/08/80 Journal Officiel p.3611, 16/09/81 Journal Officiel p.2098, 15/09/83 Journal Officiel p.3335, 18/10/85 Journal Officiel p.3277, 02/05/89 Journal Officiel p.4217, 29/08/96
F	Loi N.93-1418, 31/12/93	Journal Officiel 01/01/94, p.14
FIN	Työturvallisuuslaki 58/299, 28/6/58, muutokset 144/93 ja 509/93 Laki työsuojelun valvonnasta ja muutoksenhausta työsuojeluasioissa 131/72, uusi nimi 29/87, muutos 510/93 Valtioneuvoston päätös rakennustyön turvallisuudesta 23/6/94	
I	Decreto legislativo N.494, 14/08/96	Gazzetta Ufficiale p.24, 23/09/96
IRL	Regulations 1995	Statutory Instrument N.138, 01/06/95
L	Règlement Grand Ducal 04/11/94	Mémorial A N.96, p.1880, 17/11/94

141

NL	Wet N.440, 09/06/94 Bouwprocesbesluit N.597, 03/08/94	Staatsblad p.1, 23/06/94 Staatsblad p.1, 11/08/94
P	Decreto-lei N.155/95, 12/06/95 Portaria N.101/96, 07/03/96	Diário da República, p.4222, 01/07/95 Diário da República I série B N.80, p.703, 3/4/96
S	Arbetsmiljölag 1977:1160, 19/12/77 Arbetsmiljöförordning 1977:1166, 19/12/77	
UK	The Construction (General Provision Regulations) 1961	Statutory Instrument N.1580 of 1961
	The Construction (Lifting Operations) Regulations, 22/08/61	Statutory Instrument N.1581 of 1961
	The Construction (Working Places) Regulations 1966 (Amendment)	Statutory Instrument N.94, 1966
	The Construction (Health and Welfare) Regulations 1966	Statutory Instrument N.95, 1966
	Amendment of Regulation 1961 N1580	Statutory Instrument N.1681, 1974
	Amendment of Regulation 1961 N1580	Statutory Instrument N.1593, 1984
	Amendment of Regulation 1961 N1580	Statutory Instrument N.1657, 1988
	Amendment of Regulation 1961,	Statutory Instrument N.635 and 682,
	Amendment of Regulation 1961 N1580	Statutory Instrument N.2793, 1992
	Amendment of Regulation 1961 N1580	Statutory Instrument N.2932, 1992
	Amendment of Regulation 1966 N.94	Statutory Instrument N.1593, 1984
	Amendment of Regulation 1966 N.95	Statutory Instrument N.209, 1974
	Amendment of Regulation 1966 N.95	Statutory Instrument N.917, 1981
	Amendment of Regulation 1966 N.95	Statutory Instrument N.2966, 1992
	The Construction (Design and Management) Regulations 1994, 10/01/95	Statutory Instrument N.3140 of 1994
	The Construction (Health,Safety and Welfare) Regulations 14/06/96	Statutory Instrument (HMSO) N.1592, p.1
	Construction (Health, Safety and Welfare) Regulations (Northern Ireland) 29/10/96	Statutory Rules of Northern Ireland 1996, p 1

HEALTH AND SAFETY AT WORK - THE WORKPLACE AND CATEGORIES OF WORKERS PARTICULARLY AT RISK

Provision of health and safety signs at work

Council Directive 92/58/EEC of 24 June 1992 on the minimum requirements for the provision of health and/or safety signs at work (ninth individual Directive within the meaning of Directive 89/391/EEC).

1) Deadline for implementation of the legislation in the Member States

24.06.94

2) References

Official journal L 245, 26.08.92

A	Bundesgesetz über Sicherheit und Gesundheitsschutz bei der Arbeit Kennzeichnung sverordnung - Kenn V	Bundesgesetzblatt, S. 3785, 17/06/94 Bundesgesetzblatt 1997, Teil II nr.101, 11/4/97 p 443
B		
D	Musterbauordnung-MBO, Fassung Dezember 1993 Arbeitsstättenverordnung, 20/03/75 Unfallverhütungsvorschrift Rammen-VBG 41, 01/04/80 Unfallverhütungsvorschrift Steinbrüche, Gräbereien, VGB 42, 01/10/84 VBG 43, 01/04/84 VBG 1 - Allgemeine Vorschriften, 01/04/77	Sammlung der Einzel-Unfallverhütungsvors-chriften der gewerblichen Genossenschaften, p.1 Sammlung der Einzel-Unfallverhütungsvors-chriften der gewerblichen Genossenschaften, p.1 Sammlung der Einzel-Unfallverhütungsvors-chriften der gewerblichen Genossenschaften, p.1 Sammlung der Einzel-Unfallverhütungsvors-

		chriften der gewerblichen Genossenschaften, p.1
	VBG 4 - Elektrische Anlagen und Betreibsmittel, 01/04/79	Sammlung der Einzel-Unfallverhütungsvorschriften der gewerblichen Genossenschaften, p.1
	VBG 5 - Kraftbetriebene Arbeitsmittel, 01/10/85	Sammlung der Einzel-Unfallverhütungsvorschriften der gewerblichen Genossenschaften, p.1
	VBG 7, 01/04/77	Sammlung der Einzel-Unfallverhütungsvorschriften der gewerblichen Genossenschaften, p.1
	VBG 44 - Tragbare Eintreibgeräte, 01/04/84	Sammlung der Einzel-Unfallverhütungsvorschriften der gewerblichen Genossenschaften, p.1
	VBG 7 Nr. 6, 01/05/54	Sammlung der Einzel-Unfallverhütungsvorschriften der gewerblichen Genossenschaften, p.1
	VBG 45 - Arbeiten mit Schußapparaten, 01/04/90	Sammlung der Einzel-Unfallverhütungsvorschriften der gewerblichen Genossenschaften, p.1
	VBG 74, 01/10/92	Sammlung der Einzel-Unfallverhütungsvorschriften der gewerblichen Genossenschaften, p.1
	VBG 109 - Erste Hilfe, 01/10/94	Sammlung der Einzel-Unfallverhütungsvorschriften der gewerblichen Genossenschaften, p.1
	VBG 125, 01/04/95	Sammlung der Einzel-Unfallverhütungsvorschriften der gewerblichen Genossenschaften, p.1
	VBG 7tl, 01/05/63	Sammlung der Einzel-Unfallverhütungsvorschriften der gewerblichen Genossenschaften, p.1
	VBG 8, 01/04/80	Sammlung der Einzel-Unfallverhütungsvorschriften der gewerblichen Genossenschaften, p.1
	VBG 9, 01/12/74	Sammlung der Einzel-Unfallverhütungsvorschriften der gewerblichen Genossenschaften, p.1
	VBG 12, 01/10/90	Sammlung der Einzel-Unfallverhütungsvorschriften der gewerblichen Genossenschaften, p.1
	VBG 14, 01/04/77	Sammlung der Einzel-Unfallverhütungsvorschriften der gewerblichen Genossenschaften, p.1
	VBG 15, 01/04/90	Sammlung der Einzel-Unfallverhütungsvorschriften der gewerblichen Genossenschaften, p.1
	VBG 35, 01/04/83	Sammlung der Einzel-Unfallverhütungsvorschriften der gewerblichen Genossenschaften, p.1
	VBG 37, 01/04/77	Sammlung der Einzel-Unfallverhütungsvorschriften der gewerblichen Genossenschaften, p.1
	VBG 40, 01/04/76	Sammlung der Einzel-Unfallverhütungsvorschriften der gewerblichen Genossenschaften, p.1
	VBG 40a, 01/10/70	Sammlung der Einzel-Unfallverhütungsvorschriften der gewerblichen Genossenschaften, p.1
	Betriebsverfassungsgesetz 15060, 15/01/72	Bundesgesetzblatt I, p.13
	Schwerbehindertengesetz 15500, in der Fassung der Bekanntmachung vom 26/08/86	Bundesgesetzblatt I, p.1421
	Mutterschutzgesetz, in der Fassung der Bekanntmachung vom 18/04/68	Bundesgesetzblatt I, p.315
	Unfallverhütungsvorschrift, Sicherheits- und Gesundheits- schutzkennzeichnung - UVV 1.5, 21/06/96	
	Bergverordnung für alle bergbaulichen Betriebe	Bundesgesetzblatt I, p.1466

	(allg. Bundesverordnung - ABBergV), 23/10/95 Zweite Verordnung zur Änderung der VO zum Schutz vor gefährlichen Stoffen, 19/09/94 Gesetzbeschluß des Deutschen Bundestages, 13/6/96 VBG 125 - Unfallverhütungsvorschrift, 01/04/95 GUV 0.7 - Unfallverhütungsvorschrift, 00/09/94	Bundesrat Drucksache 427/96, 14/06/96 UVV - Sicherheits- und Gesundheits- schutzkennzeichnung am Arbeitsplatz, p.1 Bundesverband der Unfallversicherungsträger der öffentlichen Hand - BAGUV 0.7, p.1
DK	Bekendtgørelse N.646, ændret ved Lov n.220/87, 380/90, 177/93, 474/92, 373/92 og 273/91, 18/12/85 Bekendtgørelse N.570, 26/09/88 Bekendtgørelse N.584, 29/09/88 Bekendtgørelse N.1109, 15/12/92 Bekendtgørelse N.1163, 16/12/92 Bekendtgørelse N.1181-1183, 18/12/92 Bekendtgørelse N.1017, 15/12/93 Bekendtgørelse N.518, 17/06/94 Bekendtgørelse N.540, 22/01/94 Teknisk forskrift N.8, 10/10/94	Lovtidende Lovtidende, 26/09/88 Lovtidende, 29/09/88 Lovtidende S.1 Lovtidende S.1 Lovtidende S.1 Lovtidende S.1 Lovtidende, 17/06/94 Lovtidende S.1 Lovtidende S.161
E	Real Decreto número 1403/86 de 9/5/86 señalización de seguridad en los centros y locales de trabajo	Boletín Oficial del Estado N.132 de 8/7/86 p.6
EL	Décret Présidentiel N.422, 08/6/79 Décret Présidentiel N.1073, 12/09/81 Loi N. 1568/85, 11/10/85 Décret Présidentiel N.70A/88, 11/02/88 Décret Présidentiel N.225/89, 25/04/89 Décret Présidentiel N.70/90, 07/03/90 Décret Présidentiel N.105/95, 22/03/95	Journal Officiel p.1395, 15/06/79 Journal Officiel p.3611, 16/09/81 Journal Officiel p.3335, 18/10/85 Journal Officiel p.263, 17/02/88 Journal Officiel p.3277, 02/05/89 Journal Officiel p.213, 14/03/90 Journal Officiel p.3321, 10/04/95
F	Décrets N.92-322 et 92-323, 31/03/92 Décret N.92-323, 31/03/92 Décret N.92-332, 31/03/92 Arrêté relatif à la signalisation de sécurité et de santé au travail, 4/11/93	Journal Officiel, 01/04/92 Journal Officiel,N.4610, 01/04/92 Journal Officiel,N.4614, 01/04/92 Journal officiel 17/12/93, p.17581

FIN	Työturvallisuuslaki 299/58, muutos 144/93	

I	Decreto legislativo N.493, 14/08/96	Gazzetta Ufficiale p.3, 23/09/96

IRL	Regulations 1995	Statutory Instrument N.132, 29/05/95

L	Règlement Grand-Ducal, 28/03/95	Memorial p.860, 10/04/95

NL	Besluit N.530, 01/10/93 Besluit N.86, 04/02/95	Staatsblad p.1, 21/10/93 Staatsblad p.1, 21/02/95

P	Decreto-lei N.141/95, 18/05/95	Diário da República, p.3618, 14/06/95

S	Arbetsmiljölag 1977:1160, 19/12/77 Arbetsmiljöförordning 1977:1166, 19/12/77 Varselmärkning på arbetsplatser	 AFS 1992:15

UK	The Management of Health and Safety at Work, Regulations 1992	Statutory Instrument N.2051, 1992
	The Trade Union Reform and Employment Rights Act 1993 (Commencement N.3 and Transitional Provisions) Order 1994, 19/05/94	Statutory Instrument N.1365, 1994
	The Maternity Allowance and S.M. Pay Regulations 1994, 04/05/94	Statutory Instrument N.1230, 1994
	The Social Security Maternity Benefits and st. Sick Pay (Amendment) Regulations 19/05/94	Statutory Instrument N.1367, 1994
	The Maternity (Compulsory Leave) Regulations 1994, 21/09/94	Statutory Instrument N.2479, 1994
	The Management of Health and Safety at Work, Regulations 1994 (Amendment)	Statutory Instrument N.2865, 1994
	Management of Health and Safety at Work (Amendment) Regulations (Northern Ireland) 1994	Statutory Rules of Northern Ireland N.478, 1994
	The Suspension from Work (on Maternity Grounds) Order 1994	Statutory Instruments N.2930, 1994
	The Health and Safety (safety signs and signals) regulations, 18/02/96	Statutory Instruments N.341, p.1,

HEALTH AND SAFETY AT WORK - THE WORKPLACE AND CATEGORIES OF WORKERS PARTICULARLY AT RISK

Extractive industries (boreholes)

Council Directive 92/91/EEC of 3 November 1992 concerning minimum requirements for improving the safety and health protection of workers in the extractive industries (boreholes) (11th individual Directive within the meaning of Article 16(1) of Directive 89/391/EEC).

1) Deadline for implementation of the legislation in the Member States

03.11.94

2) References

Official Journal L 348, 28.11.92

A	Bergpolizeiverordnung für Elektrotechnik, ÖVE-E 18/83-Österreichische Bestimmungen für die Elektrotechnik	BGBL.N.737/96, p.4857, 20/12/96 Errichten elektrischer Anlagen im Bergbau unter Tag, 01/09/83
	ÖVE-EN 68/83-Österreichische Bestimmungen für die Elektrotechnik	Errichten elektrischer Anlagen im Bergbau unter Tag, 01/09/83
	ÖVE-E5,Teil 7/83-Österreichische Bestimmungen für die Elektrotechnik	Betrieb von Starkstromanlagen: Betrieb elektrischer Anlagen im Bergbau, 01/09/83
	Bundesgesetz über Sicherheit und Gesundheitsschutz bei der Arbeit	BGBL.N. 457/95
	Allgemeine Arbeitnehmerschutzverordnung-AVV	BGBL.N.218/83, geändert durch BGBL.N.369/94
	Allgemeine Maschinen- und Geräte-Sicherheitsverordnung AMGSV	BGBL.N.219/83, geändet durch BGBL.N.669/89
	Allgemeine Dienstnehmerschutzverordnung - ADSV	BGBL.N.265/51, geändert durch BGBL.N.290/89
	Maschinen-Schutzvorrichtungsverordnung	BGBL.N.43/61, geändert durch BGBL.N.219/83
	Berggesetz 1975, 13/05/75	BGBL.N.259
	Allgemeine Bergpolizeiverordnung, 02/04/59	BGBL.N.114
	Staubschädenbekämpfungsverordnung	BGBL.N.185/54
	Erdöl-Bergpolizeiverordnung	BGBL.N.278/37
	Bergpolizeiverordnung für die Seilfahrt, 28/11/67	BGBL.N.14/68
	Bergpolizeiverordnung für das Grubenrettungswesen, 22/12/71	BGBL.N.21/72

	Verordnung über verantwortliche Personen beim Bergbau, 11/03/83	BGBL.N.191
	Sprengmittelzulassungsverordnung für den Bergbau, 08/07/63	BGBL.N.215/63
	Kesselgesetz	BGBL.N.211/92
	Dampfkesselbetriebsgesetz-DKBG	BGBL.N.212/92
	Elektrotechnikgesetz-ETG 1992	BGBL.N.106/93
	Elektrotechnikverordnung für den Bergbau, 14/12/83	BGBL.N.12/84
	Explosionsschutzverordnung-ExSV 96	BGBL.N.252/96
	Elektro-Ex-Verordnung 1993	BGBL.N.45/94
	Niederspannungsgeräteverordnung 95	BGBL.N.51/95
	Elektromagnetische Verträglichkeitsverordnung 1995	BGBL.N.52/95
	EIEx-Betriebsmittel-Bergbau 1995	BGBL.N.53/95
	Elektrotechnikverordnung 1993 - ETV 93	BGBL.N.47/94
	Elektrotechnikverordnung 1996 - ETV 96	BGBL.N.105/96
	Bundesgesetz über das Verbot der Verwendung von Frauen zu Untertagearbeiten im Bergbau	BGBL.N.70/37
	Mutterschutzgesetz 1979	BGBL.N.221/79, geändert durch BGBL.N.434/95
	Arbeitsvertragsrechts-Anpassungsgesetz - AVRAG	BGBL.N.459/93, geändert durch BGBL.N.895/95
	Bundesgesetz über Beschäftigung von Kindern und Jugendlichen 1987	BGBL.N.599/87, geändert durch BGBL.N.257/93
	Arbeitsinspektionsgesetz 1993 - ArbIG	BGBL.N.27/93, in der Fassung der BGBL. N.871/95
	Betriebsrats-Geschäftsverordnung 1974 - BRGO 1974, 24/06/74	BGBL.N.355/74, geändert durch BGBL.N.814/93
	Arbeitsverfassungsgesetz - ArbVG, 14/12/73	BGBL.N.22/74, geändert durch BGBL.N.624/94
	Verordnung über Beschäftigungsverbote und Beschränkungen für weibliche Arbeitnehmer	BGBL.N.696/76
	Bergpolizeiverordnung über verantwortlmiche Personen-BPV-Personen	Bundesgesetzblatt 1997 Teil II N 108 p.43, 24/4/97
	Verordnung über Fachausbildung der Sicherheitskräfte (SFK-VO)	Bundesgesetzblatt 1995 N 277 21/4/95

B	Arrêté royal concernant les prescriptions minimales visant à améliorer la protection en matière de sécurité et de santé des travailleurs des industries extractives par forage, 6/1/97	Moniteur belge 12/3/97 p 5286

D	Bergverordnung für alle bergbaulichen Betriebe vom 23/10/95 Gesundheitsschutz-Bergverordnung, 31/07/91 Festlandsockel-Bergverordnung, 21/03/89 Markscheider-Bergverordnung, 19/12/86	Bundesgesetzblatt 1466 vom 03/11/95 Bundesgesetzblatt I, p.1751, Bundesgesetzblatt I, p.554, Bundesgesetzblatt I, p.2631

DK	Bekendtgørelse N.646, 18/12/85 Bekendtgørelse N.1109, 15/12/92 Bekendtgørelse N.1163, 16/12/92 Bekendtgørelse N.1181, 18/12/92 Bekendtgørelse N.290, 05/05/93 Bekendtgørelse N.518, 17/06/94 Bekendtgørelse N.561, 24/06/94 Bekendtgørelse N.867, 13/10/94 Bekendtgørelse N.923, 11/11/94 Energiministeriets Bekendtgørelse N.128, 6/3/96 Energiministeriets Bekendtgørelse N.711, 16/11/87 Energistyrelsens Bekendtgørelse N.1, 2/1/90 Energistyrelsens Bekendtgørelse N.421, 14/7/88 Energistyrelsens Bekendtgørelse N.127, 6/3/96 Energistyrelsens Bekendtgørelse N.540, 22/6/94 Energistyrelsens Bekendtgørelse N.912, 19/11/92 Energistyrelsens Bekendtgørelse N.605, 15/7/93 Energistyrelsens Bekendtgørelse N.901, 11/11/92 Energistyrelsens Bekendtgørelse N.539, 29/11/85 Energistyrelsens Bekendtgørelse N.51, 1/2/88 Energistyrelsens Bekendtgørelse N.579, 23/6/92 Lov N.292, 10/06/81	Lovtidende, 18/12/85 Lovtidende, 15/12/92 Lovtidende, 16/12/92 Lovtidende, 18/12/92 Lovtidende, 05/05/93 Lovtidende, 17/06/94 Lovtidende, 24/06/94 Lovtidende, 13/10/94 Lovtidende, 11/11/94

E	Real Decreto 150/96, 02/02/96	Boletín Oficial N.59, p.9407, 08/03/96

EL	Loi N.1568/85 du 18/10/85 Décision ministérielle 11-5e/f/17402/84 Décret présidentiel 17/96 du 18/02/96 Décret présidentiel N 177/97 du 2/7/97	Journal Officiel 177/A, p.3335 Journal Officiel N.11/A p.93 Journal officiel p.6288, 15/7/97

F	Décret N.96-73 du 24/01/96	Journal Officiel
	Décret N.94-785 du 02/09/94	Journal Officiel, p.12982, 03/09/94
	Décret N.87-501 du 01/07/87	Journal Officiel, p.7411, 07/07/87
	Décret N.95-694 du 03/05/95	Journal Officiel, p.7827, 11/05/95
	Décret N.88-1027 du 07/11/88	Journal Officiel, p.14049, 09/11/88
	Décret N.87-910 du 09/11/87	Journal Officiel, p.13219, 13/11/87
	Décret N.85-1154 du 28/10/85	Journal Officiel, p.12852, 06/11/95
	Décret N.92-1164 du 22/10/92	Journal Officiel, p.14871, 25/01/92

FIN	Työturvallisuuslaki 299/58, muutokset 144/93 ja 509/93 Laki työsuojelun valvonnasta ja muutoksenhausta työsuojeluasioissa 131/72, 16/2/73, muutos 510/93 Valtioneuvoston päästös räjäytys-ja louhintatyön järjestysohjeista 410/86	

I	Decreto legislativo N.624/96, 25/11/96	Gazetta Ufficiale N. 293, p.5, 14/12/96

IRL	Safety, Health and Welfare at Work (Extractive Industries) Regulations of 1997	Statutory Instruments N.467, 1997

L	Règlement Grand Ducal, 04/11/94	Memorial A N.96, p.1891, 17/11/94

NL	Besluit N. 434 van 17/08/95	Staatsblad
	Nadere regelen Mijnreglement 1964 en Mijnreglement continentaal plat inzake veiligheid en gezondheid van arbeiders in de winnings-industrie van 15/09/95	Staatscourant
	Regelen Mijnreglement 1964 melding bijzondere voorvallen van 17/08/95	Staatscourant 1988/166
	Regelen Mijnreglement continentaal plat 1964 bijzondere vorfallen van 17/08/95	Staatscourant 1988/166
	Nadere regelen Mijnreglement gasflessen van 5/5/67	Staatscourant 1967/94

	Nadere regelen Mijnreglement continentaal plat 1964 communicatemiddelen van 02/09/71	Staatscourant 1971/75 p.3, 10/09/71
	Nadere regelen Mijnreglement continentaal plat putbeveiliging van 07/10/70	Staatscourant 1970/201
	Nadere regelen Mijnreglement uitgangen en wegen van 09/10/85	Staatscourant 1985/202
	Nadere regelen Mijnreglement elektrische installaties,23/03/95	Staatscourant 61, p. 5, 27/03/95
	Nadere regelen Mijnreglement putbeveiliging van 16/05/67	Staatscourant 1967/100
	Nadere regelen Mijnreglement 1964 en Mijnreglement continentaal plat veiligheid - en gezondheids-documenten van 15/09/95	Staatscourant
	Nadere regelen Mijnreglement 1964 en Mijnreglement continentaal plat helikopterdekken van 25/09/95	Staatscourant 186, 26/09/95

P	Decreto-lei N.324/95, 16/10/95 Portaria N.197/96, 13/05/96	Diário da República p. 7416, 29/11/95 Diário da República I série B, N.130, p.1431, 04/06/96

S	Arbetsmiljölag 1977:1160, 19/12/77 Arbetsmiljöförordning 1977:1166, 19/12/77	

UK	Health and Safety at Work (Northern Ireland) Order 1978 N.1039, 25/07/78	Statutory Rules of Northern Ireland of 1978
	Safety Signs Regulations (Northern Ireland) 1981 N.352, 30/10/81	Statutory Rules of Northern Ireland of 1981
	Reporting of Injuries Disease and Dangerous Occurrences Regulations (Northern Ireland) 1986 N.247, 30/07/86	Statutory Rules of Northern Ireland of 1986
	Management of Health and Safety at Work Regulations (Northern Ireland) 1992 N.459, 26/10/92	Statutory Rules of Northern Ireland of 1992
	Provision and use of Work Equipment Regulations (Northern Ireland) 1993 N.19, 19/1/93	Statutory Rules of Northern Ireland of 1993
	Personal Protective Equipment at Work Regulations (Northern Ireland) 1993 N.20, 19/01/93	Statutory Rules of Northern Ireland of 1993
	Offshore Installations (Safety Regulations (Northern Ireland) N.221 1993, 04/05/93	Statutory Rules of Northern Ireland of 1993

	Offshore Installations and Pipeline Works (First-Aid) Regulations (Northern Ireland) 1993 N.323, 21/07/93	Statutory Rules of Northern Ireland of 1993
	Control of Substances Hazardous to Health Regulations (Northern Ireland) 1995, 24/02/95	Statutory Rules of Northern Ireland of 1995
	Offshore Installations and Pipeline Works (Management and Administration) Regulations N.738, 1995, 21/03/95	Statutory Instrument of 1995
	Offshore Installations (Prevention of Fire and Explosion and Energency Response) Regulations N.743 1995, 23/03/95	Statutory Instrument of 1995
	Borchole Sites and Operations Regulations 1995, 26/07/95	
	Borehole Sites and Operations Regulations (Nothern Ireland) 1995, 01/12/95	Statutory Rules of Northern Ireland of 1995, N. 491
	Mines Micellaneaus Health and Safety Provisions Regulations (Nothern Ireland), 05/10/95	Statutory Rules of Northern Ireland of 1995, N.379
	Quarries Micellaneaus Health and Safety Provisions Regulations (Nothern Ireland), 5/10/95	Statutory Rules of Northern Ireland of 1995, N.378
	Offshore Installations and wells (design and construction..) Regulations 25/03/96	Statutory Instruments, N.913, p.1

HEALTH AND SAFETY AT WORK - MINIMUM REQUIREMENTS

Extractive industries in the surface and underground

Council Directive 92/104/EEC of 3 December 1992 concerning minimum requirements for improving the safety and health protection of workers in the surface and underground extractive industries (12th individual Directive within the meaning of Article 16(1) of Directive 89/391/EEC).

1) Deadline for implementation of the legislation in the Member States

03.12.94

2) References

Official Journal L 404, 31.12.92

A	Bundesgesetz über den Bergbau, 13/05/75	Bundesgesetzblatt N.259
	Verordnung über verantwortliche Personen beim Bergbau, 11/03/83	Bundesgesetzblatt N.191
	Allgemeine Bergpolizeiverordnung, 02/04/59	Bundesgesetzblatt N.114
	Verordnung zur Bekämpfung von Staubschäden im Bergbau, 05/07/54	Bundesgesetzblatt N.185
	Bergpolizeiverordnung für die Seilfahrt, 28/11/67	Bundesgesetzblatt N.4, p.387, 12/01/68
	Bergpolizeiverordnung über das Grubenrettungswesen, 22/12/71	Bundesgesetzblatt N.8, p.415, 28/01/72
	Bergpolizeiverordnung für Elektrotechnik,	BGBL.N.737/96, p.4857, 20/12/96
	ÖVE-E 18/83-Österreichische Bestimmungen für die Elektrotechnik	Errichten elektrischer Anlagen im Bergbau unter Tag, 01/09/83
	ÖVE-EN 68/83-Österreichische Bestimmungen für die Elektrotechnik	Errichten elektrischer Anlagen im Bergbau unter Tag, 01/09/83
	ÖVE-E5,Teil 7/83-Österreichische stimmungen für die Elektrotechnik	Betrieb von Starkstromanlagen: Betrieb elektrischer Anlagen im Bergbau, 01/09/83
	Bundesgesetz über Sicherheit und Gesundheitsschutz bei der Arbeit	BGBL.N. 457/95
	Allgemeine Arbeitnehmerschutzverordnung-AVV	BGBL.N.218/83, geändert durch BGBL.N.369/94
	Allgemeine Maschinen- und Geräte-Sicherheitsverordnung AMGSV	BGBL.N.219/83, geändet durch BGBL.N.669/89
	Allgemeine Dienstnehmerschutzverordnung-ADSV	BGBL.N.265/51, geändert durch BGBL.N.290/89

	Maschinen-Schutzvorrichtungsverordnung	BGBL.N.43/61, geändert durch BGBL.N.219/83
	Berggesetz 1975, 13/05/75	BGBL.N.259
	Allgemeine Bergpolizeiverordnung, 02/04/59	BGBL.N.114
	Staubschädenbekämpfungsverordnung	BGBL.N.185/54
	Erdöl-Bergpolizeiverordnung	BGBL.N.278/37
	Bergpolizeiverordnung für die Seilfahrt, 28/11/67	BGBL.N.14/68
	Bergpolizeiverordnung für das Grubenrettungswesen, 22/12/71	BGBL.N.21/72
	Verordnung über verantwortliche Personen beim Bergbau, 11/03/83	BGBL.N.191
	Sprengmittelzulassungsverordnung für den Bergbau, 08/07/63	BGBL.N.215/63
	Kesselgesetz	BGBL.N.211/92
	Dampfkesselbetriebsgesetz-DKBG	BGBL.N.212/92
	Elektrotechnikgesetz-ETG 1992	BGBL.N.106/93
	Elektrotechnikverordnung für den Bergbau, 14/12/83	BGBL.N.12/84
	Explosionsschutzverordnung-ExSV 96	BGBL.N.252/96
	Elektro-Ex-Verordnung 1993	BGBL.N.45/94
	Niederspannungsgeräteverordnung 95	BGBL.N.51/95
	Elektromagnetische Verträglichkeitsverordnung 1995	BGBL.N.52/95
	EIEx-Betriebsmittel-Bergbau 1995	BGBL.N.53/95
	Elektrotechnikverordnung 1993 - ETV 93	BGBL.N.47/94
	Elektrotechnikverordnung 1996 - ETV 96	BGBL.N.105/96
	Bundesgesetz über das Verbot der Verwendung von Frauen zu Untertagearbeiten im Bergbau	BGBL.N.70/37
	Mutterschutzgesetz 1979	BGBL.N.221/79, geändert durch BGBL.N.434/95
	Arbeitsvertragsrechts-Anpassungsgesetz - AVRAG	BGBL.N.459/93, geändert durch BGBL.N.895/95
	Bundesgesetz über Beschäftigung von Kindern und Jugendlichen 1987	BGBL.N.599/87, geändert durch BGBL.N.257/93
	Arbeitsinspektionsgesetz 1993 - ArbIG	BGBL.N.27/93, in der Fassung der BGBL. N.871/95
	Betriebsrats-Geschäftsverordnung 1974 - BRGO 1974, 24/06/74	BGBL.N.355/74, geändert durch BGBL.N.814/93
	Arbeitsverfassungsgesetz - ArbVG,14/12/73	BGBL.N.22/74, geändert durch BGBL.N.624/94
	Verordnung über Beschäftigungsverbote und Beschränkungen für weibliche Arbeitnehmer	BGBL.N.696/76
	Bergpolizeiverordnung über verantwortlmiche Personen-BPV-Personen	Bundesgesetzblatt 1997 Teil II N 108 p.43 24/4/97
	Verordnung über Fachausbildung der Sicherheitskräfte (SFK-VO)	Bundesgesetzblatt 1995 N 277 21/4/95

B	Arrêté royal modifiant l'arrêté royal du 10/1/79 relatif à la politique de prévention et aux organes de sécurité, d'hygiène et d'embellissement des lieux de travail concernant les mines, les minières et les carrières souterraines, 11/4/96	Moniteur belge 22/5/96

D	Bergverordnung für alle bergbaulichen Betriebe vom 23/10/95 Gesundheitsschutz-Bergverordnung, 31/07/91 Festlandsockel-Bergverordnung, 21/03/89 Markscheider-Bergverordnung, 19/12/86	Bundesgesetzblatt 1466 vom 03/11/95 Bundesgesetzblatt I, p.1751, Bundesgesetzblatt I, p.554 Bundesgesetzblatt I, p.2631

DK	Bekendtgørelse N.646, 18/12/85 Bekendtgørelse N.1109, 15/12/92 Bekendtgørelse N.1163, 16/12/92 Bekendtgørelse N.1181, 18/12/92 Bekendtgørelse N.290, 05/05/93 Bekendtgørelse N.518, 17/06/94 Bekendtgørelse N.561, 24/06/94 Bekendtgørelse N.867, 13/10/94 Bekendtgørelse N.923, 11/11/94	Lovtidende, 18/12/85 Lovtidende, 15/12/92 Lovtidende, 16/12/92 Lovtidende, 18/12/92 Lovtidende, 05/05/93 Lovtidende, 17/06/94 Lovtidende, 24/06/94 Lovtidende, 13/10/94 Lovtidende, 11/11/94

E	Real Decreto por el que se aprueban las disposiciones mínimas destinadas a proteger la seguridad y salud de los trabajadores en las actividades mineras, 5/9/97	Boletín Oficial del Estado p.29154, 7/10/97

EL	Décret ministerielle APD7/A/F1/14080/732, 22/08/96	Journal Officiel Volume I, p.8079, 28/08/96

F	Décret N.59-285, 27/01/59 Décret N.51-508, 04/05/51 Décret N.95-694, 03/05/95 Arrêté relatif aux prescriptions minimales pour la signalisation de sécurité et de santé, 24/07/95 Arrêté relatif aux registres etplans à établir et tenir	Journal Officiel, 13/02/59 Journal Officiel, 06/05/51 Journal Officiel p.7827, 11/05/95 Journal Officiel p.12235, 15/08/95 Journal Officiel p.12003, 10/08/95

à jour, 24/07/95	
Circulaire relative à l'application du décret 95-694, 03/05/95	Journal Officiel p.7855, 11/05/95
Décret N.80-331, 07/05/80	Journal Officiel p.1183, 10/05/80
Décret N.84-146, 27/02/84	Journal Officiel p.742, 01/03/84
Décret N.87-699, 21/08/84	Journal Officiel 21/08/87
Circulaire relative à l'application du décret 84-147, 13/02/84	Journal Officiel p.2116, 01/03/84
Décret N.94-785, 02/09/94	Journal Officiel p.12982, 03/09/94
Circulaire relative à l'application du décret 94-785, 02/09/94	Journal Officiel p.12989, 08/09/84
Décret N.87-501, 01/07/87	Journal Officiel p.7411, 07/07/87
Circulaire relative à l'application du décret 87-501, 01/01/87	Journal Officiel p.7414, 07/07/87
Décret N.88-1027, 07/11/88	Journal Officiel p.14049, 09/11/88
Circulaire relative à l'application du décret 88-1027, 07/11/88	Journal Officiel p.14055, 09/11/88
Décret N.92-1164, 22/10/92	Journal Officiel p.14871, 25/01/92
Circulaire relative à l'application du décret 92-1164, 22/10/92	Journal Officiel p.14879, 25/10/92
Décret N.91-986, 23/09/91	Journal Officiel p.12613, 27/09/91
Circulaire relative à l'application du décret 91-986, 23/09/91	Journal Officiel p.12629, 27/09/91
Décret N.85-1154, 28/10/85	Journal Officiel p.12852, 06/11/95
Circulaire relative à l'application du décret 85-1154, 28/10/85	Journal Officiel p.12857, 06/11/85
Décret N.87-910, 09/11/87	Journal Officiel p.13219, 13/11/87
Circulaire relative à l'application du décret 87-910, 09/11/87	Journal Officiel p.13221, 13/11/87
Décret N.80-330, 07/05/80	Journal Officiel p.1179, 10/05/80
Décret N.95-695, 09/05/95	Journal Officiel p.7839, 11/05/95

FIN	Työturvallisuuslaki 58/299, 28/6/1958, muutokset 93/144, 29/1/93 ja 509/93 Laki työsuojelun valvonnasta ja muutoksenhausta työsuojeluasioissa 73/131, 16/2/73 Valtioneuvoston päästös räjäytys-ja louhintatyön järjestysohjeista 86/410	

I	Decreto legislativo N.624/96, 25/11/96	Gazetta Ufficiale N. 293, p.5, 14/12/96

IRL	Safety, Health and Welfare at Work (Extractive Industries) Regulations of 1997	Statutory Instruments N.467, 1997

L	Règlement Grand Ducal, 04/11/94	Memorial A N.96, p.1903, 17/11/94

NL	Arbeidsomstandighedenbesluit N.602 Winningsindustrie en dagdouw, 29/07/94	Staatsblad, p.1, 16/08/94

P	Decreto-lei N.324/95, 16/10/95 Portaria N.198/96, 13/05/96	Diário da República p. 7416, 29/11/95 Diário da República I série B N.130, p.1437, 04/06/96

S	Arbetsmiljölag 1977:1160, 19/12/77 Arbetsmiljöförordning 1977:1166, 19/12/77	

UK	Safety Signs Regulations (Northern Ireland) 1981 N.352, 30/10/81	Statutory Rules of Northern Ireland of 1981
	Reporting of Injuries Disease and Dangerous Occurrences Regulations (Northern Ireland) 1986 N.247, 30/07/86	Statutory Rules of Northern Ireland of 1986
	Management of Health and Safety at Work Regulations (Northern Ireland) 1992 N.459, 26/10/92	Statutory Rules of Northern Ireland of 1992
	Provision and use of Work Equipment Regulations (Northern Ireland) 1993 N.19, 19/1/93	Statutory Rules of Northern Ireland of 1993
	Personal Protective Equipment at Work Regulations (Northern Ireland) 1993 N.20, 19/1/93	Statutory Rules of Northern Ireland of 1993
	Control of Substances Hazardous to Health Regulations (Northern Ireland) 1995, 24/2/95	Statutory Rules of Northern Ireland of 1995
	Mines Micellaneaus Health and Safety Provisions Regulations 1995, 26/07/95	
	Quarries Micellaneaus Health and Safety	

Provisions, 26/07/95	
Borehole Sites and Operations Regulations (Nothern Ireland) 1995, 01/12/95	Statutory Rules of Northern Ireland of 1995, N.491
Mines Micellaneaus Health and Safety Provisions Regulations (Nothern Ireland), 05/10/95	Statutory Rules of Northern Ireland of 1995, N.379
Quarries Micellaneaus Health and Safety Provisions Regulations (Nothern Ireland), 5/10/95	Statutory Rules of Northern Ireland of 1995, N.378
Borehole Sites and Operations Regulations (Nothern Ireland) 1995, N. 491, 21/12/95	
Mines Micellaneaus Health and Safety Provisions Regulations(Nothern Ireland), N.379, 05/10/95	
Quarries Micellaneaus Health and Safety Provisions Regulations (Nothern Ireland), N.378, 05/10/95	

HEALTH AND SAFETY AT WORK - THE WORKPLACE AND CATEGORIES OF WORKERS PARTICULARLY AT RISK

Fishing vessels

Council Directive 93/103/EC of 23 november 1993 concerning the minimum safety and health requirements for work on board fishing vessels (10th individual Directive within the meaning of article 16(1) of Directive 89/391/EEC).

1) Deadline for implementation of the legislation in the Member States

23.11.1995

2) References

Official Journal L 307, 13.12.1993

A	Not applicable	

B		

D	Sechste Verordnung zur Anderung der Lebensmittel-Kennzeichnungsverordnung vom 28/3/95 Unfallverhütungsvorschriften für unternehmen der Seefahrt (UVV-SEE) Stand 1/1/92 Elfter nachtrag zu den Unfallverhütungsvors-chriften für Unternehmen der Seefahrt 30/7/96 Neufassung der Schiffsicherheits Verordnung 21/10/94 geändert durch VO von 14/6/96 Seetagebuchverordnung SeeTgbV, 8/2/85	BGBL Nr 19 vom 20/4/95 s.502 Bundesgesetzblatt 1985 Teil I N.7, 15/2/85 p.306

	Verordnung über die Unterbringung der Besatzungsmitglieder an Bord von Kauffahrteischiffen 8/2/73	Bundesgesetzblatt 1973 Teil I N.10, 10/2/73 p.66
	Schiffsoffizier - Ausbildung Verordnung	Bundesgesetzblatt Teil I N.2, 21/1/92 p.23
	Schiffmechaniker - Ausbildung Verordnung 12/4/94	Bundesgesetzblatt 1994 Teil I N.23, 21/4/94 p.797
	Schiffsbesetzungs Verordnung 4/4/84	Bundesgesetzblatt 1984 Teil I N.17, 11/4/84 p.523
	Verordnung über die Krankenvorsorge auf Kauffahrteischiffen, 25/4/72	Bundesgesetzblatt 1972 Teil I N.38, 29/4/752 p.734
	Verordnung über die hygienischen Anforderungen an Fischerzeugnisse und lebende Muscheln 31/4/94	Bundesgesetzblatt 1994 Teil I, 19/4/94 p.737

DK	Søfartstyrelsens tekniske forskrift E, 22/12/95	
	Bekendtgørelse af lov om skibes sikkerhed, 2/5/95	Lovtidende A, p.1374, 15/01/95
	Bekendtgørelse 713/87, 11/11/87	
	Bekendtgørelse 528/95, 26/06/95	Lovtidende A, 15/01/96
	Søfartstyrelsens tekniske forskrift 2/91, 03/09/91	
	Bekendtgørelse 504/94, 13/06/94	Lovtidende A, 15/01/96
	Søfartstyrelsens tekniske forskrift 3/95, 07/04/95	
	Søfartstyrelsens tekniske forskrift 8/94, 10/10/94	
	Søfartstyrelsens tekniske forskrift 7/92, 15/12/92	

E	Real Decreto N 930/95	Boletín oficial del Estado del 20/7/95, p.22286
	Real decreto 1216/97 por el que se establecen las disposiciones mínimas de seguridad y salud en el trabajo a bordo de los busques de pesca (18/7/97)	Boletín oficial del Estado N 188, del 7/8/97, p.24070

EL	Décret présidentiel N.281	Journal Officiel Volumen I, p.3885

F	Décret N. 84-810 du 30/08/84, Annexe 226-6-02 et 217-4-05	
	Code du travail (Art.L742-5,L231-8, L231-8-1,L231-8-2,L231-9,Art.9	
	Arrêté du 29/07/92, portant modification du Règlement annexé à l'Arrêté du 23/11/87 relatif à la sécurité des navires	
	Arrêté du 23/11/87, Annexe 217-3-02,Art. 51 et 51-1	

Code du travail (Art.L230-1 à L230-4)	
Arrêté du 11/02/94 portant création et fixant les conditions de délivrance du brevet d'aptitude à l'exploitation des embarcations et radeaux de sauvetage	
Code du travail, Art.L231-3-1, Art. R231-32 à R231-45)	
Décret N.85-378 27/03/85	
Décret N.91-1187 20/11/91	
Arrêté du 16/04/86 modifié relatif aux conditions d'aptitude physique à la profession de marin à bord des navires	
Art. 221-7-02S et 221-07-03S du Réglement sur la securité des navires annexé à l'arrêté du 23/11/87	
L'Arrêté du 12/04/88 relatif à l'organisation des examens pour l'obtention des certificats, diplômes et brevets de la marine marchande	
L'Arrêté du 24/07/91 modifié relatif aux conditions de formation professionnelle	
Arrêté du 09/07/92 relatif au programme d'enseignement médical dans la formation professionnelle maritime	Journal Officiel, 28/07/92, p.10134
Arrêté du 22/02/94 modifiant l'arrêté du 09/07/92 relatif au programme d'enseignement médical dans la formation professionnelle maritime	Journal Officiel, 08/03/94, p.3695
Arrêté N. 354 GM2/IGEM 26/03/93 modifiant l'arrêté du 12/08/86 relatif à l'examen pour l'obtention du certificat de capacité	
Arrêté N.1314 GM2/IGEM 22/10/92 relatif à l'examen pour l'obtention du brevet de lieutenant de pêche	
Arrêté N.4455 GM2 DU 26/12/85 relatif à l'examen de patron de pêche	
L'Arrêté N.238 GM2/IGEM 01/03/91 relatif à l'examen pour l'obtention du brevet de pêche	
L'Arrêté du 12/08/86 relatif à l'examen pour l'obtention du certificat de capacité	
Arrêté portant modification de l'arrêté du 23/11/87 relatif à la sécurité des navires, 20/12/95	
Articles L230-1 à L230-4, L231-3-1, L231-8, L238-8-1, L231-8-2, L231-9, L236-1 à L236-13, L742-5, R231-32 à R231-45, R742-8-1 à R742-8-13 du Code du Travail	
Décret N.84-810 30/08/84 Art.9	
Annexe 226-6-02 et 217-4-05 du Règlement annexé à l'arrêté du 23/11/87 (pris en application du décret N.84-810)	

FIN	Valtioneuvosten päätös N:0 1329, 23/11/95	
	Valtioneuvosten päätös N:0 1328, 23/11/95	
	Työturvallisuuslaki 1958/299, 28/06/58	Yrityksen Lakikanta, seurattu SDK 307/96, 9.työlainsäädäntö, p.1
	Laki työsuojelun valvonnasta ja muutoksenhausta työsuojeluasioissa 1973/131, 16/02/73	Yrityksen Lakikanta, seurattu SDK 307/96, 9.työlainsäädäntö, p.1
	Työsopimuslaki 1970/320, 30/04/70	Yrityksen Lakikanta, seurattu SDK 307/96, 9.työlainsäädäntö, p.1
	Vuosilomalaki 1973/272, 30/03/73	Yrityksen Lakikanta, seurattu SDK 307/96, 9.työlainsäädäntö, p.38
	Työterveyshuoltolaki 1978/743, 29/09/78	Yrityksen Lakikanta, seurattu SDK 307/96, 9.työlainsäädäntö
	Laki yhteistoiminnasta yrityksissä 1978/725, 22/09/78	Yrityksen Lakikanta, seurattu SDK 307/96, 9.työlainsäädäntö
	Laki miesten ja naisten välisestätasa-arvosta 1986/609, 08/08/86	Yrityksen Lakikanta, seurattu SDK 307/96, 9.työlainsäädäntö
	Asetus työsuojelun valvonnasta 1973/954, 21/12/73	
	Valtioneuvoston päätös n.o 418, 11/06/81	
	Valtioneuvoston päätös n.o 417, 11/06/81	
	Valtioneuvoston päätös henkilösuojaimista 1993/1406, 22/12/93	Yrityksen Lakikanta, seurattu SDK 307/96, 9.työlainsäädäntö
	Valtioneuvoston päätös työvälineiden turvallisesta käytöstä n:o 1403, 22/12/93	Suomen säädöskokoelma 1993 n:o 1403-1405, p.3659, 28/12/93
	Valtioneuvoston päätös työpaikkojen turvamerkeisttä ja niiden käytöstä 1994/976, 10/11/94	Yrityksen Lakikanta, seurattu SDK 307/96, 9.työlainsäädäntö, p.1

I		

IRL	EC (Dangerous substances) Regulations of 1994	SI N.77 of 1994

L	Not applicable	

NL	Besluit houdende wijziging van het Vissersvaartuigenbesluit van 01/09/95 Besluit houdende vastellning van het tijdstip van inwerkingtreding van het besluit van 01/09/95	Staatsblad N.456, p.1 van 03/10/95 Staatsblad N.516, p.1 van 31/10/95

P	Portinaria N.956/95 de 7/8/95 Decreto-Lei N 116/97 22/4/97	Diário da República, N.181 de 7/8/95, p.4958 Diário da República I série A 12/5/97

S	Sjölag, 09/06/94 Fartygssäkerhetslag, 28/01/88 Sjöfartsverkets kungörelse om fartyg med obemannat maskinrum, 12/06/70 Sjöfartsverkets kungörelse om elektrisk anläggning och utrustning på fartyg, 20/07/71 Sjöfartsverkets kungörelse om brandskydd på fartyg, 12/06/70 Gasolkungörelse, 25/06/63 Sjöfartsverkets kungörelse om ändring i sjöfartsstyrelsens kungörelse med föreskrifter om fartygs utrustning, 16/06/70 Sjöfartsverkets kungörelse om lyftinrättningar på fartyg, 17/05/73 Sjöfartsverkets kungörelse om bostäder och ekonomilokaler m.m. på fartyg, 19/05/70 Sjöfartsverkets kungörelse med föreskrifter och allmänna råd om sjukvård och apotek på fartyg, 02/02/94 Sjöfartsverkets kungörelse med föreskrifter om fartygs stabilitet och fribord, 07/04/93 Sjöfartsverkets kungörelse med bemannings- och vakthållningsföreskrifter för vissa fiskefartyg 02/12/83	SFS 94:1009, 28/06/94 SFS 88:49, 16/02/88 Sjöfartsverkets Meddelanden, S.A , N.9, 25/06/70 Sjöfartsverkets Meddelanden, S.A , N.15, 18/8/71 Sjöfartsverkets Meddelanden, S.A , N.13, 25/6/70 Kungliga Sjöfartsstyrelsens Meddelanden, S.A, N.10, 08/07/63 Sjöfartsverkets Meddelanden, S.A , N.16, 13/7/70 Sjöfartsverkets Meddelanden, S.A , N.9, 07/06/73 Sjöfartsverkets Meddelanden, S.A , N.4, 03/06/70 SJÖF 94:6, 18/03/94 SJÖF 93:3, 30/06/93 SJÖF 83:57, 09/12/83

UK	Fishing Vessel (Safety Provisions) Rules 6/3/75	Statutory Instruments 1975/330 p 887

HEALTH AND SAFETY AT WORK - MINIMUM REQUIREMENTS

Organization of working time

Council Directive 93/104/EC of 23 November 1993 concerning certain aspects of the organization of working time.

1) Deadline for implementation of the legislation in the member states

23.11.1996

2) References

Official Journal L 307, 13.12.1993

A	Arbeitszeitgesetz (AZG)	Bundesgesetzblatt N.461/1969 idF BGBl. I Nr.46/1997
	Arbeitsruhegesetz (ARG)	Bundesgesetzblatt N.144/1983 idF BGBl. N.46/1997
	Bäckereiarbeiter / Innengesetz (Bäck AG)	Bundesgesetzblatt N.410/1996
	Krankenanstalten-Arbeitszeitgesetz (KA-AZG)	Bundesgesetzblatt N.8/1997
	Urlaubsgesetz (URlG)	Bundesgesetzblatt N. 390/1976, idF BGBl. N.832/1995
	Bauarbeiter-Urlaubs -und Abfertigungsgesetz (BUAG)	Bundesgesetzblatt N.414/1972, idF BGBl. N.754/1996
	Schauspielergesetz (SchauspG)	Bundesgesetzblatt N.144/1922, idF BGBl N.624/1994
	Hausbesorgergesetz (HBG)	Bundesgesetzblatt N. 16/1970, idF BGBl. N.833/1992
	Landarbeitsgesetz (LAG)	Bundesgesetzblatt N.287/1984, idF BGBl. N.514/1994
	Nachtschwerarbeitsgesetz (NSchG)	Bundesgesetzblatt N.354/1981, idF BGBl. N.473/1992
	Verordnung über die Gesundheitsüberwachung am Arbeitsplatz (VGÜ)	Bundesgesetzblatt II N.27/1997
	Arbeitsnehmerschutzgesetz (ASchG)	Bundesgesetzblatt N.450/1994, idF BGBl. I N.9/1997
	Arbeitsinspektionsgesetz (ArbIG)	Bundesgesetzblatt N.27/1993, idF BGBl. I N.63/1997

	Ärztegesetz (ÄrzteG)	Bundesgesetzblatt N.373/1984, idF BGBl. N.752/1996

B	Loi relative au travail de nuit/Wet betreffende de nachtarbeid 17/2/97	Moniteur belge / Belgisch Staatsblad 8/4/97 p 8145

D	Gesetz vom 06/07/94	Bundesgesetzblatt Teil I, 10/07/94, p.1170
	Gesetz vom 30/07/96	Bundesgesetzblatt Teil I, 05/08/96, p.1186
	Verordnung vom 24/09/74	Bundesgesetzblatt Teil I, p. 2356
	Verordnung vom 25/11/94	Bundesgesetzblatt Teil I, p. 3512, 02/12/94
	Richtlinie für den betriebstechn. und sicherheitstechn. Dienst in den Verwaltungen und Berieben des Bundes, 28/01/78	Gemeinsames Ministerialblatt N.7/1978, p.114
	Arbeitszeitverordnung-AZVO, 29/01/96	Gesetzblatt für Baden-Württemberg, p.76
	Urlaubsverordnung-UrlVO 29/01/96	Gesetzblatt für Baden-Württemberg, p.481, 1986
	Verordnung der Landesregierung über die Lehrverpflichtung an Kunsthochschulen, 15/02/82	Gesetzblatt für Baden-Württemberg, N.4, p.49, 26/02/82
	Verordnung der Landesregierung über die Lehrverpflichtungen an Universitäten, päd. Hochschulen u. Fachhochschulen, 11/12/95	Gesetzblatt für Baden-Württemberg, N.2, p.43, 12/01/96
	Verordnung über die Arbeitszeit f. den bayerischen öffentlichen Dienst	Gesetzblatt für Bayern N.17, 1995, p.409
	Bekanntmachung des Bayerischen Staatsministeriums der Finanzen vom 25/04/96	Amtl. Mitteilungsblatt des Bayerischen Staatsministeriums der Finanzen N.10, 07/06/96, p.258
	Bekanntmachung der Neufassung der Urlaubsverordnung, 10/08/920	Bayerisches Gesetz- und Verordnungsblatt N.17, 1990, p.366
	Neunte Änderung zur Urlaubsvordnung, 11/02/92	Gesetzblatt für Bayern N.3, 1992, p.18
	Zehnte Änderung zur Urlaubsvordnung, 20/06/95	Gesetzblatt für Bayern N.15, 1995, p.302
	Vorl. Richtlinien über die Gewährleistung eines arbeitsmedizinisch. sicherheitstech. Arbeitsschutzes in der staatl. Verwaltung des Freistaates von Bayern, 18/12/81	Bayr. Staatsanzeiger N.53
	Verordnung über die Arbeitszeit von Beamten, 21/11/95	Gesetz- und Verordnungsblatt für Berlin N.70, 30/11/95, p.790
	Verordnung über den Erholungsurlaub der Beamten und Richter,	Gesetz- und Verordnungsblatt für Berlin p.775
	Verordnung zur Änderung mutterschutz und urlaubsrechtlicher Vorschriften vom 12/12/91	Gesetz- und Verordnungsblatt für Berlin N.55, 20/12/91, p.286
	Verordnung zur Änderung arbeits und urlaubsrechtlicher Vorschriften vom 28/08/95	Gesetz- und Verordnungsblatt für Berlin N.50, 7/9/95,
	Verordnung über die Arbeitszeit von Beamten, 10/10/94	Gesetz- und Verordnungsblatt für das Land Brandenburg, N.70, 28/10/94, p.908

1. Verordnung zur Änderung der VO über den Erholungsurlaub der Beamten und Richter, 7/10/96	Gesetz- und Verordnungsblatt für das Land Brandenburg
Verordnung über die Arbeitszeit von Beamten, 29/09/59	Gesetzblatt der Freien Hansestadt Bremen, p.138
Grundsätz für die gleitende Arbeitszeit, 04/05/95	Gesetzblatt der Freien Hansestadt Bremen, p.449
Verwaltungsordnung über die Arbeits- und Dienstzeit, 25/09/74, zuletzt geändert am 28/03/89	Gesetzblatt der Freien Hansestadt Hamburg
Verordnung über den Erholungsurlaub der hamburgischen Beamten, 22/02/72	Gesetzblatt der Freien Hansestadt Hamburg, P.45
Verordnung über die Arbeitszeit von Beamten idF. vom 14/03/89	Gesetzblatt p.91
Verordnung zur Änderung mutterschutz, urlaubs- und arbeitszeit- rechtlicher Vorschriften, 17/09/96	Gesetz- und Verordnungsblatt für Hessen N.22, 02/10/96, p.385
2. Verordnung zur Änderung der Verordnung über die Arbeitszeit von Justizvollzugsanstaltsbeamten, 26/04/89	Gesetz- und Verordnungsblatt für Hessen N.8, 17/05/89, p.125
Verordnung über die Arbeitszeit d. hessischen Polizeivollzugseamtin-nen u. Beamten, 24/05/93	Gesetz- und Verordnungsblatt für Hessen N.14, 16/06/93, p.191
Verordnung über den Urlaub der Beamten im Lande Hessen idF. vom 16/11/82	Gesetz- und Verordnungsblatt für Hessen p.82, 1985
Verordnung über die Arbeitszeit von Beamten, 17/04/95	Gesetzblatt für das Land Mecklenburg-Vorpommern N.8, p.224, 1995
Niedersächsisches Beamtengesetz in der Fassung vom 11/12/85, zuletzt geändert durch das Gesetz vom 01/04/96	Niedersächsisches Gesetz- und Verordnungsblatt p.82
Bekanntmachung der Neufassung der Verordnung über die Arbeitszeit von Beamten, 16/02/90	Niedersächsisches Gesetz- und Verordnungsblatt N.10, 23/02/90, p.69
6. Verordnung zur Änderung der Verordnung über die Arbeitszeit von Beamten, 10/04/91	Niedersächsisches Gesetz- und Verordnungsblatt N.16, 12/04/91, p.169
10. Verordnung zur Änderung der Verordnung über die Arbeitszeit von Beamten, 19/06/96	Niedersächsisches Gesetz- und Verordnungsblatt N.11, 26/06/96
2. Gesetz zur Änderung dienstrechtlicher Vorschriften, 20/11/95	Niedersächsisches Gesetz- und Verordnungsblatt N.21, 24/11/95
Verordnung über die Arbeitszeit der Beamten des Feuerwehrdienstes der Gemeinden und Landkreise, 27/11/86	Niedersächsisches Gesetz- und Verord-nungsblatt N.41, 14/03/96
Bekanntmachung der Neufassung der Verordnung über die Arbeitszeit der Lehrkräfte an öffentl. Schulen 13/08/92, geänd. d. VO vom18/07/96	Niedersächsisches Gesetz- und Verordnungsblatt N.33, 25/08/92
Bekanntmachung der Neufassung des niedersächsischen Hochschulgesetz, 21/01/94	Niedersächsisches Gesetz- und Verordnungsblatt N.2, 26/01/94, p.13
Verordnung über die Lehrverpflichtung an Hochschulen, 18/01/96	Niedersächsisches Gesetz- und Verordnungsblatt N.2, 1996, p.20
Verordnung über die niedersächs. Fachhochschule für Verwaltung und Rechtspflege, 10/02/96	Niedersächsisches Gesetz- und Verordnungsblatt N.3, 27/02/96, p.26
Bekanntmachung der Neufassung des Beschlusses des Landesministeriums über die Arbeitszeit in der	Niedersächsisches Ministerialblatt N.6, 1990, p.127

Landesverwaltung, 20/12/89	
Verordnung über den Erholungsurlaub der Beamten und Richter, 02/10/90	Gesetz- und Verordnungsblatt für Niedersachsen N.37, 05/10/90, p.444
Bekanntmachung der Neufassung der Verordnung über die Arbeitszeit von Beamten, 28/12/86	Gesetz- und Verordnungsblatt für Nordrhein-Westfalen, 1987, p.15
13. Verordnung zur Änderung der Verordnung über die Arbeitszeit von Beamten, 30/07/96	Gesetz- und Verordnungsblatt für Nordrhein-Westfalen N.32, 08/08/96, p.244
Verordnung über die Arbeitszeit der Polizeivollzugsbeamten, 15/08/75	Gesetz- und Verordnungsblatt für Nordrhein-Westfalen p.532
4. Verordnung zur Änderung der Verordnung über die Arbeitszeit von Polizeivollzugsbeamten, 17/8/96	Gesetz- und Verordnungsblatt für Nordrhein-Westfalen N.40, 05/09/96, p.348
Bekanntmachung der Neufassung der Verordnung über den Erholungsurlaub der Beamten und Richter, 14/09/93	Gesetz- und Verordnungsblatt für Nordrhein-Westfalen, p.690
Arbeitszeitverordnung, 23/03/93	Gesetz- und Verordnungsblatt für Rheinland-Pfalz, p.152
Landesverordnung über den Urlaub der Beamten in der Fassung vom 17/03/71	Gesetz- und Verordnungsblatt für Rheinland-Pfalz, p.125
Verordnung über die Arbeitszeit von Beamten, 19/11/62	Gesetz- und Verordnungsblatt für das Saarland, p.787
Verordnung über die Arbeitszeit von Polizeivollzugsbeamten,	Gesetz- und Verordnungsblatt für das Saarland, N.35, 25/08/78, p.737
Bekanntmachung der Neufassung der Verordnung über den Erholungsurlaub der Beamten und Richter, 08/12/70	Gesetz- und Verordnungsblatt für das Saarland, N.41, 28/12/70, p.978
Neufassung der Allgemeinen Verwaltungsvorschriften zur Durchführung der gesetzlichen Unfallversicherung durch die Landesausführungsbehörde für Unfallversicherung, 20/05/92	Gemeinsames Ministerialblatt des Saarlandes, 10/08/92, p.190
Verordnung der Sächsischen Staatsregierung über die Arbeitszeit der Beamten, 12/01/93	Gesetz- und Verordnungsblatt für das Land Sachsen N.5, 10/02/93, p.75
Verordnung der Sächsischen Staatsregierung über den Urlaub der Beamten und Richter, 01/02/93	Gesetz- und Verordnungsblatt für das Land Sachsen N.9, 05/02/93, p.123
Verordnung über die Arbeitszeit von Lehrkräften an öffentlichen Schulen, 18/02/92	Gesetz- und Verordnungsblatt für das Land Sachsen-Anhalt N.8, 28/02/92, p.128
Verordnung über die Arbeitszeit von Beamten des Justizvollzugsdienstes, 29/05/95	Gesetz- und Verordnungsblatt für das Land Sachsen-Anhalt N.18, 06/06/95, p.146
Verordnung über die Arbeitszeit des Polizeivollzugsdienstes, 26/10/94	Gesetz- und Verordnungsblatt für das Land Sachsen-Anhalt N.48, 04/11/94, p.978
Verordnung über die Arbeitszeit der Beamten, 07/05/92	Gesetz- und Verordnungsblatt für das Land Sachsen-Anhalt N.18, 21/05/92, p.324
Verordnung über den Urlaub von Beamten, 09/11/93	Gesetz- und Verordnungsblatt für das Land Sachsen-Anhalt N.49, 12/11/93, p.688
Verordnung über den Urlaub von Beamten und Richtern, 30/09/94,	Gesetz- und Verordnungsblatt für den Freistaat Thüringen N.32, 11/10/94, p.1095
Verordnung über die Arbeitszeit der Beamten,	Gesetz- und Verordnungsblatt für den Freistaat

	12/04/95 Landesverordnung über die Arbeits-zeit der Beamten in der Fassung vom 16/01/87 Bekanntmachung der Neufassung der Verordnung über den Erholungsurlaub der Beamten und Richter, 28/01/87 Landesverordnung zur Änderung der Erholungsurlaubs-, Mutterschutz- und Erziehungsurlaubsverordnung, 02/08/96	Thüringen N.9, 11/05/95, p.192 Gesetz- und Verordnungsblatt für das Land Schleswig-Holstein N.3, 04/02/87, p.42 Gesetz- und Verordnungsblatt für das Land Schleswig-Holstein N.4, 10/02/87, p.53 Gesetz- und Verordnungsblatt für das Land Schleswig-Holstein N.16, p.572
DK	Arbejdsmiljøloven Bekendtgørelse N 867 af 13/10/94 om arbejdets udførelse Bekendtgørelse N 1282 af 20/12/96 om hvileperiode og fridøgn mv (bkg 1282/96) nedenfor kaldet bekendtgørelse Lov N 286 af 24/4/96 om brug af helbredsoplysninger mv på arbejdsmarkedet , nedenfor kaldet Helbredsloven Lov om ferie, jf lovbekendtgørelse N 102 af 3/3/93 med de ændringer, der følger af lov N 415 af 1/6/93	
E	Ley N.8/80, 10/03/80 Real Decreto N.2001/83, 28/07/83 Ley N.11/94, 19/05/94 (11610)	Boletín Oficial del Estado, 14/3/80 N.64 Boletín Oficial del Estado, 29/7/83 N.180 Boletín Oficial del Estado, 23/5/94 N.122, p.15805
EL		
F		
FIN	Työaikalaki (605/96), 09/08/96	Suomen Saeaedöskokoelma 1996, p.1637

I		

IRL	Organisation of Working Time Act, 7/5/97	

L		

NL	Wet van 23/11/95 Besluit van 04/12/95 Besluit van 04/12/95	Staatsblad N. 598 van 1995 Staatsblad N. 599 van 1995 Staatsblad N. 600 van 1995

P		

S	Lag om ändring i arbetstidslagen (1982:673) Arbetstidslag Lag om arbetstid m.m. i husligt arbete Semesterlag Arbetsmiljölag Arbetsmiljöförordning	Svensk författningssamling (SFS) 1982:673 Svensk författningssamling (SFS) 1996:360 Svensk författningssamling (SFS) 1970:943 Svensk författningssamling (SFS) 1977:480 Svensk författningssamling (SFS) 1977:1160 Svensk författningssamling (SFS) 1977:1166

UK		

RIGHTS AND PROTECTION OF CHILDREN AND ADOLESCENTS

Protection of young people at work

Council Directive 94/33/EC of 22 June 1994 on the protection of young people at work.

1) Deadline for implementation of the legislation in the Member States

22.06.1996

2) References

Official Journal L 216, 20.08.1994

A	Kundmachung der Salzburger Landesregierung vom 6/12/95 über die Wiederverlautbarung der Salzburger Landarbeitsordnung Bundesgesetz: Änderung des Bundesgesetzes über die Beschäftigung von Kindern und Jugendlichen 87 und des Allgemeinen Sozialversicherungs-gesetzes 1/7/97	Landesgesetzblatt für Salzbourg, Nr.7/96 Bundesgesetzblatt für die Republik Österreich N.79/97 ausgegeben am 14/7/97 s.1073

B	Loi du/Wet van 21/03/95 relative au travail des étudiants et des jeunes travailleurs	Moniteur Belge/Belgisch Staatsblad van 21/04/95

D	Zweites gesetz zur Änderung des Jugendarbeitsschutzgesetzes vom 24/2/97	Bundesgesetzblatt Teil I vom 27/2/97 Seite 311

DK	Bekendtgørelse N.711 af 16/11/87 om sikkerhed m.v.på havanlæg. Energiemin 4612-1	Lovtidende A af 16/11/87
	Bestemmelser BL 6-20	Stetens Luftfartvæsen udgave 4, 18/06/90
	Bestemmelser BL 6-30	Stetens Luftfartvæsen udgave 3, 18/06/90
	Bestemmelser om certifikat som kabinebesætnings-medlem, CA-certifikat, hherunder grunduddannelse	Stetens Luftfartvæsen udgave 2, 18/06/90
	Arbetsministeriets lovgekendtgørelse N.184 af 22/03/95	
	Lov N. 458 af 12/06/96 om ændring af lov om arbetsmiljø	Lovtidende A af 12/06/96, hæfte 90, p.2523
	Arbetsministeriets lovgekendtgørelse N.516 af 14/06/96 om ungesarbejde	Arbejdsmin.j. N.1995-2160-16
	Arbetsministeriets lovgekendtgørelse N.867 af 13/10/94 om arbejdsudførelse	Arbejdsmin.j. N.1992-5332-1
	Arbetsministeriets lovgekendtgørelse N.562 af 16/12/85 om arbejde med metallisk bly og dettes ionforbindelser	Arbejdsmin.j. N.1985-3240-62
	Arbetsministeriets lovgekendtgørelse N.660 af 24/09/86 om asbest.	Arbejdsmin.j. N.1986-3240-60
	Lov N. 77 af 31/01/94	Lovtidende A af 31/01/94
	Søfatsstyrelsens bekendtgørelse N.662 af 05/07/96 om unges arbejde i sskibe	Erhversmin., Søfartsstyrelsen j.N.4101 -2, Lovtidende A af 05/07/96, p.3912
	Sømandslovens, jf. lovbekendtgørelse N.766 af 19/09/95	
	Industrieministeriets bekendtgørelse N.400 af 07/06/89	Industrimin.j.N.89-7619-1
	Søfatsstyrelsens bekendtgørelse N.523 af 31/06/93 om ændring af bekendtgørelse om lægeundersøgelse af søfarende	Industrimin., Søfartsstyrelsen, Arbejdsmiliøkontoret j. N.4101-6
	Søfatsstyrelsens Tekniske forstkrift N. 2 af 07/04/95 om sikkerhedsarbejde i handelsskibe	Arbejdsmiliøkontoret j. N.4400-2
	Søfatsstyrelsens Tekniske forstkrift N. 7, 15/12/92 om sikkerhed og sundhed for arbeijde i skibe	Arbejdsmiliøkontoret j. N.4101-11

E	Ley N. 31/1995	Boletin Oficial del Estado N.269, 10/11/95, p.32590
	Real Decreto N.1435/85, 01/08/85	Boletin Oficial del Estado, 14/08/85
	Real Decreto legislativo N.2/95, 07/04/95	Boletin Oficial del Estado N.86, 11/4/95, p.10695
	Real Decreto legislativo N.1/95, 24/03/95	Boletin Oficial del Estado N.75, 29/3/95, p.9654

EL		

F		

FIN	Laki nuorista työntekijösistä (998/93), muutos (408/96) Merityöaikalaki (296/76) Laki työajasta kotimaanliikenteen aluksissa (248/82) Asetus nuorten työntekijöiden suojelusta annetun asetuksen muuttamisesta (755/96), 18/10/96 Työministeriön päätös nuorille työntekijöille vaarallisesta töistä (756/96), 25/10/96	

I		

IRL	Protection of Young Persons (Employment) Act of 26/06/96	Statutory Instruments N.16/1996
	Enterprise and Employment (Delegation of Ministerial Functions), Order of 1996	Statutory Instruments N.349/1996
	Protection of Young Persons (Employment) Act (Commencement), Order of 1996	Statutory Instruments N.371/1996
	Protection of Young Persons(Employment) (Exclusion of Workers in the Fishing/Shipping sectors), Regulations of 1997	Statutory Instruments N.1/1997
	Protection of Young Persons (Employment of Close Relatives), Regulations of 1997	Statutory Instruments N.2/1997
	Protection of Young Persons(Employment) (Prescribed Abstract), Regulations of 1997	Statutory Instruments N.3/1997
	Terms of Employment (Information) Act, 1994 (Section 3(6)), Order of 1997	Statutory Instruments N.4/1997

L		

NL	Arbeidstijden wet Besluit van 15/1/97 houdende regels in het belang van de veiligheid, de gesondheid en het welzijn in verband met de arbeid (Arbeidsomstandigheden-besluit) Arbeidsomstandighedenregeling (Arboregeling) van 7/3/97	Staatsblad nummer 598 van 23/11/95 Staatsblad nummer 60 van 97 Staatscourant nummer 63

P	Decreto-Lei n°26/94 - segurança, higiene e saúde no trabalho, 1/2/94 Decreto-Lei n°441/91, 14/11/91 Decreto-Lei n°715/93, 3/8/93 Lei n°7/95 - Segurança, higiene e saúde no trabalho, 29/3/95 Decreto-Lei n°396/91, 16/10/91 Decreto-Lei n°397/91, 16/10/91 Decreto-Lei n°398/91, 16/10/91 Decreto-Lei n°49408 - Aprovação do novo regime do contrato individual de trabalho - revogação da legislação anterior em tudo o que for contrário disposições do presente diploma, designadamente do decreto-lei n°47032, 21/11/64 Decreto-Lei n°409/71 - Duração e organização do tempo de trabalho, 22/9/71 Decreto-Lei n°410/71 - Duração do tempo de trabalho, 22/9/71 Decreto-lei n°874/76 - Prestação do tempo de trabalho, 9/12/76 Lei de Bases do sistema educativo N°46/86 24/7/86	Diario da República n°480, I serie A, 1/32/94 pp 4173-4175 Diario da República n°262, 14/11/91, pp 5826-5833 Diario da República n°180, I serie B, 3/8/93 pp 4173-4175 Diario da República n°75, I serie A, 29/3/95 pp 1710-1713 Diario da República n°238, 16/10/91, pp 5367-5370 Diario da República n°238, 16/10/91, pp 5370-5373 Diario da República n°238, 16/10/91, p.5373 Diario do Governo n°275, I serie, 24/11/69 Diario do Governo 27/9/71 Diario do Governo 27/9/71 Diario do Governo n°300, 28/12/76, pp 2856-2860 Diario da República n°237, 14/10/86, pp3067-3081

S	Arbetarskyddsstyrelsens föreskrifter om minderåriga 6/6/96	Arbetarskyddsstyrelsens författningssamling (AFS) 1996:1, 15/7/96

UK	The Children and Young Persons Act of 1933	
	The Children and Young Persons Act of 1963	
	The Children (Performances) Regulations of 1968	Statutory Instruments N.1728 of 1968
	The Merchant Shipping Act of 1995	
	The Health and Safety (young Persons) Regulations of 23/1/1997	Statutory Instruments N.135 of 1997, pp.1710-1713, 23/1/97

PUBLIC HEALTH - CANCER

Labelling of tobacco products

Council Directive 89/622/EEC of 13 November 1989 on the approximation of the laws, regulations and administrative provisions of the Member States concerning the labelling of tobacco products and the prohibition of the marketing of certain types of tobacco for oral use.

Council Directive 92/41/EEC of 15 May 1992 amending Directive 89/622/EEC on the approximation of the laws, regulations and administrative provisions of the Member States concerning the labelling of tobacco products and the prohibition of the marketing of certain types of tobacco for oral use.

1) Deadline for implementation of the legislation in the Member States

Directive 89/622/EEC: 01.07.1990

Directive 92/41/EEC: 01.07.1992

2) References

Official Journal L 359, 08.12.1989

Official Journal L 158, 11.06.1992

A	Bundesgesetz über das Herstellens und das Inverkehrbringen von Tabakzeugnissen sowie die Werbung für tabakzeugnisse und den Nichtraucherschutz (Tabakgesetz)	Bundesgesetzblatt für die Republik Österreich Nr 431/95, 30/6/95

B	Arrêté Royal du/Koninklijk Besluit van 13/08/90 Arrêté Royal du/Koninklijk Besluit van 14/04/93	Moniteur Belge du/Belgisch Staatsblad van 05/01/91, p.117 Moniteur Belge du/Belgisch Staatsblad van 23/06/93, p.15248

D	Verordnung (Tabak THmv) vom 29/10/91	Bundesgesetzblatt, 1991, Teil 1 N.61, 08/11/91, S.2053

DK	Lov N.426, 13/06/90 Bekendtgørelse N.507, 28/06/90 Bekendtgørelse N.1213, 23/12/92	Lovtidende A S.1394, 13/06/90

E	Real Decreto N.510/1992, 14/05/92	Boletín Oficial del Estado N.133, 3/6/92, p.1881

EL	Décision Ministérielle N.A2Y/2160 du 29/11/90 Décision Ministérielle N.Y3/2917/92 du 27/05/93	Journal Officiel N.781, Volume B, p.9092, 12/12/90 Journal Officiel N.435, p.4804, 16/06/93

F	Loi N.91.32, 10/01/91 Arrêté du 26/04/91 Loi N.94 - 43 du 18/01/94	Journal officiel, 12/01/91, p.615 Journal officiel, 05/05/91, p.6047 Journal officiel, 19/01/94, p.960

FIN	Laki toimenpiteistä tupakoinnin vähenttämiseksi N.693/76, 13/08/76 muutos N.953/92 Asetus toimenpiteistä tupakoinnin vähenttämiseksi N.255/77, 25/02/77 muutos N.1502/92 Sociali-ja terveysministeriön päätös tupakkatuotteiden vähittäismyyntipakkausten merkinnöistâ ja nikotiinin mittausmenetelmistä N.1504/92, 23/12/952 Landskapslag om ändring av landskapslagen om åtgärder för begränsning av tabakrökningen N.44/94, 19/05/94 Laki tupakoinnin vähentämiseksi annetun lain muuttamisesta 765/94, 19/8/94	

I	Decreto Inter Ministeriale del 31/07/90 Decreto Ministeriale del 16/07/91 Decreto Ministeriale del 26/07/93 Legge N.146 del 22/02/94	Gazzetta Ufficiale N.198, p.8, 25/08/90 Gazzetta Ufficiale N.201, p.8, 28/08/91 Gazzetta Ufficiale N.230, p.11, 30/09/93 Supplemento Ordinario della Gazzetta Ufficiale N.39, 04/03/94

IRL	Regulations 1991 Regulations 1994	Statutory Instrument N.326 of 1991 Statutory Instrument N.28 of 1994

L	Règlement Grand Ducal, 19/06/90 Règlement Grand Ducal, 21/07/92 Loi, 06/01/95	Memorial A, N.30, p.411, 30/06/90 Memorial A, N.58, p.1902, 01/08/92 Memorial A, N.1, 13/01/95

NL	Besluit van 15 september 1994 tot uitvoering van Artikel 2, erste lid, van de Tabaksinet Besluit van 15/09/94 tot wijziging van het Aandvidingb. Tabakprodukten	Staadsblad 718 van 11/10/94, p.1 Staatsblad N.719, 1994

P	Decreto-lei N.200/91, 29/05/91 Portaria N.821/91, 12/08/91 Decreto-lei N.386/93, 18/11/93 Portaria N.32/94, 11/01/94	Diário da República I Serie A, N.123, p.2950, 29/05/91 Diário Da República I Serie B, N.184, p.4086, 12/08/91 Diário Da República I Serie A, N.270, p.6440, 18/11/93 Diário Da República I Serie B, N.8, p.110, 11/1/94

S	Tabakslag Förordning am ändring i Förordningen (1985:796) med vissa bemyndiganden för Socialstyrelsen att meddela föreskrifter m.m. Socialstyrelsen att meddela föreskrifter Varningtester och innehållsdeklaration på tobaks-varor samt begränsning av tjärhalten i cigaretter Förordning om förbud mot export av snus,	Svensk författningssamling 1993:581 Svensk författningssamling 1993:583 Socialstyrelsens författningssamling (SOFS) 1994:9 Svensk författningssamling (SFS) 1994:1266

UK	Regulations 1991 Tobacco for Oral Use (Safety) Regulations 1992 Regulations 1993	Statutory Instrument N.1530 of 1991 Statutory Instrument 1992 Statutory Instrument N.1947 of 1993

178

PUBLIC HEALTH - CANCER

Maximum tar yield of cigarettes

Council Directive 90/239/EEC of 17 May 1990 on the approximation of the laws, regulations and administrative provisions of the Member States concerning the maximum tar yield of cigarettes.

1) Deadline for implementation of the legislation in the Member States

18.11.91

2) References

Official Journal L 137, 30.05.90

A	Bundesgesetz über das Herstellen und das Inverkehrbringen von Tabakzeugnissen sowie die Werbung für Tabakzeugnisse und den Nichtraucherschutz (Tabakgesetz)	Bundesgesetzblatt für die Republik Österreich Nr.431/95, 30/6/95

B	Arrêté Royal du/Koninklijk Besluit van 13/08/90	Moniteur Belge du/Belgisch Staatsblad van 05/01/91, p.117

D	Verordnung vom 29/10/91	Bundesgesetzblatt I N.61, S.2053, 08/11/91

DK	Lov N.426, 13/06/90 Bekendtgørelse N.507, 28/06/90	

E	Real Decreto N.192/88, 04/03/88	Boletín Oficial del Estado, 9/3/88, p.7499
	Real Decreto N.510/92, 14/05/92	Boletín Oficial del Estado, 3/6/92, p.18815, N.133

EL	Décision Ministérielle N.A2C/5259 du 21/12/91	Journal Officiel N.57, Volume B, p.518 du 5/2/92

F	Arrêté ministériel, 26/04/91	Journal Officiel p.6047, 05/05/91

FIN	Valtionovoston päästös tupakkatuotteen haitta-aineiden enimmäismääristä 1502/92, 23/12/92	

I	Legge N.142, 19/02/92 (Art. 37)	Gazzetta Ufficiale N.42, 20/02/92, p.22

IRL	European Communities (Tar yield of Cigarettes) Regulations 1991	Statutory Instrument N.327 of 1991

L	Règlement Grand Ducal, 19/06/90	Memorial A, N.30, p.411, 30/06/90

NL	Besluit Teergehalte sigaretten	Staatsblad N.256, 14/04/94

P	Portaria N.821/91, 12/08/91	Dario da Républica I Serie B N.184, p.4086, 12/8/91

S	Tobakslag, Förordning om ändring i förordningen (1985:796) med vissa bemyndiganden för Socialtyrelsen att meddela föreskrifter m.m.	Svensk författningssamling (SFS) 1993:581 Svensk författningssamling (SFS) 1993:583

UK	Regulations 1992	Statutory Instrument N.2783 of 1992

RECAPITULATIVE TABLE

RECAPITULATIVE TABLE

DIRECTIVES	B	DK	D	EL	E	F	IRL	I	L	NL	A	P	FIN	S	UK
I. LABOUR LAW															
75/129 Collective redundancies	C	C	C	C	C	C	C	C	C	C	C	C	C	C	C
77/187 Transfers of undertakings	C	C	C	C	C	C	C	C	C	C	C	C	C	C	C
80/987 Insolvency of the employer (+ 87/164)	C	C	C	C	C	C	C	C	C	C	C	C	C	C	C
91/533 Information of the employees	C	C	C	C	C	C	C	C	C	C	C	C	C	C	C
92/56 Collective redundancies 2	C	C	C	C	C	C	C	C	C	C	C	C	C	C	C
94/45 European works councils	C	C	C	C	C	C	C	C	N	C	C	N	C	C	-
96/71 Posting of workers (deadline: 16.12.1999)	-	-	-	-	-	-	-	-	-	-	-	-	-	-	-
II. EQUAL TREATMENT															
75/117 Equal pay	C	C	C	C	C	C	C	C	C	C	C	C	C	C	C
76/207 Access to employment	C	C	C	C	C	C	C	C	C	C	C	C	C	C	C
79/7 Social security	C	C	C	C	C	C	C	C	C	C	C	C	C	C	C
86/378 Occupational social security schemes	N	N	C	C	C	C	C	C	N	N	C	C	C	C	C
86/613 Self-employed women	C	C	C	C	C	C	C	C	C	C	C	C	C	C	C
92/85 Pregnant workers	C	C	C	IC	C	C	C	C	N	C	C	C	C	C	C
96/34 Parental leave (deadline: 3.6.1998)	C	-	-	-	-	-	-	-	-	C	-	-	-	-	-
96/97 Occupational social security schemes 2	N	N	N	N	N	N	C	N	N	N	C	C	N	C	C
III. FREE MOVEMENT OF WORKERS															
64/221 Special measures	C	C	C	C	C	C	C	C	C	C	C	C	C	C	C
68/360 Abolition of restrictions on movement	C	C	C	C	C	C	C	C	C	C	C	C	C	C	C
72/194 Right to remain in the territory of a Member State	C	C	C	C	C	C	C	C	C	C	C	C	C	C	C
IV. HEALTH AND SAFETY AT WORK															
78/610 Vinyl chloride monomer	C	NR	C	C	C	C	NR	C	C	C	C	C	C	C	C
80/1107 Chemical, physical and biological agents	C	C	C	C	C	C	C	C	C	C	C	C	C	C	C
82/130 Explosive atmospheres (firedamp)	C	C	C	C	C	C	NR	C	C	C	C	NR	NR	NR	C
82/605 Metallic lead	C	C	C	C	C	C	C	C	C	C	C	C	C	C	C
83/477 Asbestos	C	C	C	C	C	C	C	C	C	C	C	C	C	C	C

	DIRECTIVES	B	DK	D	EL	E	F	IRL	I	L	NL	A	P	FIN	S	UK
86/188	Noise	C	C	C	C	C	C	C	C	C	C	C	C	C	C	C
88/35	Explosive atmospheres (firedamp) 2	C	C	C	C	C	C	NR	C	C	C	C	NR	NR	NR	C
88/364	Banning of agents and other activities	C	C	C	C	C	C	C	C	C	C	C	C	C	C	C
88/642	Chemical, physical and biological agents 2	C	C	C	C	NR	C	C	C	C	C	C	NR	C	C	C
89/391	Framework	C	C	C	C	C	C	C	C	C	C	C	C	C	C	C
89/654	Workplaces	C	C	C	C	C	C	C	C	C	C	C	C	C	C	C
89/655	Work equipment	C	C	C	C	C	C	C	C	C	C	C	C	C	C	C
89/656	Personal protective equipment	C	C	C	C	C	C	C	C	C	C	C	C	C	C	C
90/269	Manual handling of loads	C	C	C	C	C	C	C	C	C	C	C	C	C	C	C
90/270	Display screen equipment	C	C	C	C	C	C	C	C	C	C	C	C	C	C	C
90/394	Carcinogens	C	C	C	C	C	C	C	C	C	C	C	C	C	C	C
90/679	Biological agents	C	C	C	C	C	C	C	C	C	C	C	C	C	C	C
91/269	Explosive atmospheres (firedamp) 3	C	C	C	C	C	C	C	C	C	C	C	NR	NR	NR	C
91/322	Chemical, physical and biological agents 3	C	C	N	N	N	N	C	C	C	N	C	NR	C	C	C
91/382	Asbestos 2	C	C	C	C	C	C	C	C	C	C	C	C	C	C	C
91/383	Temporary employment	C	C	C	C	C	C	C	C	C	C	C	C	C	C	C
92/29	Medical assistance on board of vessels	N	C	C	C	C	C	N	N	N	C	C	C	C	C	C
92/57	Construction	C	C	C	C	C	C	C	C	C	C	C	C	C	C	C
92/58	Health and safety signs	C	C	C	C	C	C	C	C	C	C	C	C	C	C	C
92/91	Drilling	C	C	C	C	C	C	C	C	C	C	C	C	C	C	C
92/104	Mining	C	C	N	N	C	N	N	N	N	C	C	N	C	C	N
93/88	Biological agents 2	C	C	C	C	C	C	C	C	C	C	C	C	C	C	C
93/103	Work on board fishing vessels	N	C	C	C	C	C	N	N	NR	C	NR	C	C	C	C
93/104	Working time	C	C	C	C	C	N	C	N	N	C	C	N	C	C	N
94/33	Young people	C	C	C	C	C	N	C	N	N	C	IC	C	C	C	IC
94/44	Explosive atmospheres (firedamp) 4	C	C	C	C	C	C	NR	C	C	C	C	NR	NR	NR	C
95/30	Biological agents 3	C	C	N	C	C	C	N	N	N	C	N	C	C	C	C
95/63	Work equipment 2 (deadline: 5.12.1998)	-	-	-	-	C	-	-	-	C	-	C	-	-	C	-
96/94	Chemical, physical and biological agents 4 (deadline: 1.6.1998)	-	-	-	-	-	-	-	-	-	-	-	-	-	-	-
97/42	Carcinogens 2 (deadline: 27.6.2000)	-	-	-	-	-	-	-	-	-	-	-	-	-	-	-
97/59	Biological agents 4 (deadline: 31.3.1998)	-	-	-	-	-	-	-	-	-	-	-	-	-	-	-
97/65	Biological agents 5 (deadline: 30.6.1998)	-	-	-	-	-	-	-	-	-	-	-	-	-	-	-

	DIRECTIVES	B	DK	D	EL	E	F	IRL	I	L	NL	A	P	FIN	S	UK
	V. PUBLIC HEALTH															
89/622	Labelling	C	C	C	C	C	C	C	C	C	C	C	C	C	C	C
90/239	Maximum tar yield	C	C	C	C	C	C	C	C	C	C	C	C	C	C	C
92/41	Labelling 2	C	C	C	C	C	C	C	C	C	C		C	C	C	C
	% of national legislation communicated 1.1.1998	92	96	96	90	96	92	94	90	84	94	96	96	98	100	96

Average 15 Member States: 94.2 %

C: Communication of national legislation
N: No communication of national legislation
NR: Directive not relevant to a particular country
IC: Incomplete communication

European Commission

National transposition measures — Situation at 1st January 1998

Luxembourg: Office for Official Publications of the European Communities

1998 — 187 pp. — 21 x 29.7 cm

ISBN 92-828-2747-X

Price (excluding VAT) in Luxembourg: ECU 15